"This is a powerful book. Esperide has produced a text that is both poetic and informative, designed to help us understand the potential of our present through the prism of past lives. She expands our sense of time in a way that honors ancestral wisdom and modern physics. Time is an intelligence that molds us by encompassing future, present and past into one interconnected continuum dedicated to our growth and awareness."

— Jim Garrison, *PhD* Founder/President Ubiquity University

"This book has the potential to take you into altered states of consciousness. It is potent and timely as the structures of modernity and certainty, especially scientific materialism are collapsing on the weight of their own hubris. New/ancient/emerging ways of knowing, being, sensing and relating to the world will continue to (re)emerge. This is the time of the trans-rational, where the whispers of ancestors, deep time intuition, forgotten memories, archetypal deities, ancestral forces, and the teachings of plants are as valid as reductionist consensus-making methodologies."

— Alnoor Ladha, Co-author "*Post Capitalist Philanthropy: The healing of wealth in the time of collapse*."

"In this expansive book, Esperide takes us on a journey through time reflected in brilliantly told stories of the human experience. Filled with vast and varied colors of life experience, these stories awaken the remembrance of a deeper individual and collective knowing that we exist in many distinct identities in many places in time. "33 Lives from the Book of Time" will expand your perspective of the life you are living today. And you will emerge with greater understanding, compassion and love for yourself and of all life.

Thank you Esperide for writing this sacred work; it is a gift for humanity."

— Julie Piatt /SriMati, Spiritual Guide of Water Tiger and founder of SriMu

"The richness of both philosophical and scientific arguments gives Esperide's work a credibility that leads the reader to question the certainties acquired according to the canons of materialistic life that governs our world. It offers us the refreshing idea that there could be a reality very different from the hopeless one in which we live. These thirty-three stories, so uplifting to humanity, are the perfect representation of this."

— Patrick Djivas, Musician and composer, universally recognized as a precursor of the modern electric bass.

"This is a book that gives us back precious memories. Reading the stories of these lives you find yourself floating between dreaming and remembering. Esperide offers us keys to understand the breadth of our soul, and what it means to be citizens of time. Her insights are useful to help us remember how precious we are. This is a valuable inspirational piece toward the recomposition of the human soul."

— Antilope Verbena, Healer and Teacher at Damanhur University.

"Esperide's new book, '33 Lives from the Book of Time' took me on a powerful personal journey through different times and into different living realities. Each story... a life, a death, a time... stirred deep memories and ignited waking dreams through which I could sense my own greater story... my soul's story. An entertaining, yet magical book to read."

— Jennifer Evanko, Spiritual Mentor, Host of *Adventures in Consciousness*.

ESPERIDE ANANAS AMETISTA

33 LIVES from the BOOK of TIME

STORIES AND SCIENCE
TO REMIND YOU WHO YOU ARE

DAMANHUR

Esperide Ananas Ametista (Silvia G. L. Buffagni)

33 LIVES FROM THE BOOK OF TIME

ISBN: 978-88-7012-160-5

2st edition DHORA Srl,
Impresa Sociale - Vidracco (Turin), Italy

Printed in Italy in May 2023

INDEX

To Addax Melograno, a great teacher.
And to my parents, who gave me life
within this timeline.

STORIES THAT ARE *OUR STORIES*

Foreword by David Pearl

Since we humans first sheltered from the storm in caves or clustered around our fires on the vast savanna we've used stories to help us make meaning of what's happened and to imagine what's next.

Today, the technology may have changed—cave paintings and runes have given way to videos and social media—but our fascination with story is undimmed.

Though stories are, I believe, intended to teach us about ourselves and the world we live in, we increasingly use them to escape reality. Think of the countless hours a large part of humanity spends watching Netflix, to brighten what feels like the boredom of everyday life—or the sense of being imprisoned in pandemic lockdowns. There's a huge industry that uses narrative to transport us out of our lives and encourage us into fantasies.

I think you'll find the stories Esperide introduces you to here do the opposite. They direct attention right back to ourselves. I don't want to be a spoiler for what lies ahead but I think you'll discover these stories are not just about us, *they are* our stories.

You'll also notice they are not conventional tales, with standard plots laden with baddies, goodies, difficulties and resolutions. They are lives captured in rich but spare language, with much left unsaid. This is intentional. It allows us, the readers, to meet the text halfway, sensing into the ambiguities to provide our answers and details.

The art historian Ernst Gombrich talked of the "beholders' share," *whereby the observer's is asked to meet the painter's images halfway and add their own interpretation to bring an artwork to life. There is a similar invitation to collaborate here; to bring your own perspective to the stories; to add the detail almost as if you were drawing on your memory. Because, and this is another potential spoiler, you* are.

The ideas Esperide introduces us to in this book, particularly in the second half, fundamentally challenge conventional understanding of time and place. I find myself asking "is what's past is truly gone? How many lives do we live?

Have I lived some of yours and you some of mine? And what would time look like if we could step outside it?"

I have known Esperide Ananas Ametista for many years (who knows, maybe forever*) and her mind tends to have this effect on me. And those she teaches. Constantly stretching our understanding of* what is, *and encouraging us to be creative about* what could be.

For a nomadic creative like me meeting her for the first time felt like reuniting with an old friend. So when, a few months later, I heard the she and some of her fellow Damanhurians were holding a workshop in London, I signed up without checking the title. Any time spent with these folk was sure to be fascinating.

When I realized it was about meeting another "me" *somewhere else across time, I was curious. But also skeptical. I found my thinking truly stretched. Yet, what I learned in those two, enriching days helped me understand this life I was living and what I might want to do with it.*

As I say, I entered my first experience not sure I believed in past lives. You may feel the same as you start this book. But as Esperide explained there was and is no obligation to believe *in anything.*

Only to be open and explore. So, drawing on my background as a performing artist and writer, I treated it as a creative exercise. But as my story emerged, the sort of story you will be reading here, the experience began to feel more like an act of remembering. Parts of a puzzle fell into place and a life emerged—my life, a life I had lived previously, and I am still living somewhere in another time—in three dimensional depth and rich colour.

And what a story.

The life that revealed itself was strikingly like my current one. A creative man, a singer, poet, musician who made his living in and around Moldavia in the eighteenth century fashioning wooden toys for children. When he died—and I realized I remembered that death—he left a warm imprint on the community who would tell stories about him. These morphed over time into a regional (and less sinister) version of the well known Pied Piper fable.

This story—I think of it more as my personal—has stayed with me through the years, offering nudges, precedents and guidance as I have created and staged artistic, developmental experiences around the world. Often with children, but always with the child inside the adult.

At the end of the workshop another participant walked up to me with an outstretched hand. On it was a green tinged, glassy lump of rock. "I felt compelled to bring this to the workshop," *he said.* "And I didn't know why until I heard your story." *He explained it was moldavite, a mineral which originates, as the name suggests in Moldavia.* "It's been in my house for a long while but - I think this is for you".

I was touched as he passed the precious stone into my hand. And as I am again now, reading the stories in this book. They leave me certain we are more connected than we imagine in more ways than we can dream.

We've been trying to persuade Esperide to write this book of past life stories for ages. It's a thrill that she now has.

For me, the book loosens up the deadening hold of so-called reality on our thinking, so we can be more creative with the lives we are living, have lived, and will live in future. But whether you are a "believer" *in past lives, a skeptic, an intellectual explorer or simply curious, I think you'll find it fascinating to spend time with these stories— these lives.*

Finally, I just want to say the fact that you are holding this book in your hand right now, reading this text at this moment means: "I think this is for you."

David Pearl
artist, performer, business&innovation consultant, author of "*Stories for Leaders*", founder of the social enterprise Street Wisdom.
London, June 2022

BEDTIME STORIES TO REMIND YOU WHO YOU ARE

Introduction by the Author

This is primarily a book of stories, not a treatise on reincarnation, although in the second part of the book I present contemporary scientific discoveries that seem to provide a framework to explain it. I chose those I found most interesting as they offered new perspectives. I hope you will find them intriguing and mind-opening just as I did.

Imagine time as a territory where you can travel in all directions. Just as on a map of planet Earth the mountains of Europe exist alongside the Amazon rainforest, the deserts of North Africa and the great oceans, so too on the map of time, all epochs would be present simultaneously: the thirty-three lives recounted in this book were waiting to be found so that they can pulsate again, like a living light, along the roads of time. They may awaken memories of your presence in other places and times, and give you strength and inspiration for your life now.

Creativity and trust, I believe, are precious tools for the survival of our very humanity, in these challenging times when an incessant plethora of news and voices pervades the space of our life, trying to confine our thoughts within the same tracks. They want to trick us into reacting emotionally in favor, or against, whatever the situation may be. A push towards a constant duality that restricts our creativity and actions. Yet, these times of transformation require us to broaden our perspectives, and find new keys of interpreting events.

Focusing on something drastically different, on the edge of the possible—something that may be the synthesis of the life journeys of all of us—can be an act of radical liberation of the mind. These are stories of lives really lived, in other points in time, by women and men who now inhabit our era. They hold the energy of emotions, of challenges, of choices really made. For this reason, they also belong to those whom, reading them, feel a resonance, like the calling of an ancient and familiar voice. A breath of fresh air for the spirit so that, with a touch of humor and enchantment, you can embrace new emotions and ideas.

1

THIRTY-THREE LIVES FROM THE BOOK OF TIME

1.1 Why These Stories?

We live to enrich our palette of emotions, knowledge, relationships, and connections to others and life. We've all had adventurous, happy, and serene lives, as well as difficult existences with trauma and suffering. Sometimes the very latter help to understand the value of life, or to complete cycles of experience. But these are not the existences I've chosen to recount. This is not a book of therapy, it's a book of healing and spiritual awakening to help you reconnect to the voices of your soul.

These lives—that I have selected among many others—tell the story of our adventure on this Planet in a different way from what we learn in school. In some existences, the experiences and choices made have epic, universal traits and shed light into the depths of the soul. They help us remember that we are not here to be alone, but to find comfort, love and growth in and with others.

Other stories transport us to times of transition, where the world order changes, and characters face difficult choices in order to protect what they hold dear. The echoes of these lives are similar to the Zeitgeist of the period in which we live now.

The first life in this book is about Love. Not as a feeling or a passion, but as the highest strategy aimed at recomposing the human soul. It is the story told by a being who came to Earth from the stars and, with his people, started a new line of evolution. A plan to bring about a communion of all Life, while preserving the memory of the uniqueness of the experience lived by each being. A path from the complete merging of minds and emotions to the intoxication of individuality, to finally reach a new level of connection; a link made more vibrant by the different experiences of everyone.

The lives I've chosen to share take place on our precious Earth, but not all of the protagonists inhabit bodies like the ones we have today. Some come from distant planets, others have in them parts of the consciousness of the plant world, which for millennia was a conscious component of the human soul.

These stories, at times, have the flavor of fairy tales; listening to them can trigger memories so ancient and unusual as to connect us to a Plan of evolution that can give new meaning to our long human history. Perhaps fairy tales are also a way of remembering what is true, yet today is no longer part of what we consider possible.

Other tales in this book recount the lives of men and women like us, in this precious vehicle that is our body. Human beings who made important choices and who, with their stories, help us sense how the material world is intertwined with that of the spirit: we can always draw strength and inspiration from it.

1.2 Lives are ... All at Once

I've been able to track down these lives because their "signal" is still active in time. And if the transmission is still going on, it's because at some point in time these people are still alive. To understand this paradox, you can imagine time as if it were a territory. An instant would correspond to a space, and all instants could therefore be present at the same time. Just as the territories from where you find yourself now to the other end of the world exist all at once. From your place of observation you can't see all of them, but if you flew over the Earth in an airplane, little by little they would all appear.

From the perspective of the moment that is today, if we consider time only as a line, these stories recount lives already ended. But in the dimension where time is all present, these people are living right now. These stories are already in the Book of Time, and it's as if someone was writing them down right now. Each life is intertwined with all the others, everything is present in the territory of time.

1.3 Memory is a Power

We live in an era that seems suspended between an old paradigm that is shattering—intensifying control, inequality, and de-humanization—and the possibility of a time of Awakening. Two opposing lines of probability, two timelines that fluctuate, come together, alternate. According to widely accepted quantum physics research, it is up to us to manifest the one we want to live on, by focusing our attention on it, and cultivating the emotions that make us feel the event we desire has already happened. Finding the key to our memories creates a different relationship with the most hidden dimension of time, the one in which it is alive and sentient.

We could then change events not only as we observe them, but because we become aware that we too are part of the forces that create time as the great connecting fabric and container of all life's experience. Memories of existences so different from our own in this age, like those in these stories, can give us strength, help us heal from the diseases of powerlessness and lack of meaning. They inspire new insights to find/build our way to a joyful collective evolution. Memory is a power.

1.4 Lives... and Death

Our ways of feeling, thinking, and loving change from era to era, from place to place; the search for meaning, leaving a legacy and making a difference to others and the world, are values always present in the human heart. All of these stories testify to a journey of awareness toward understanding one's mission, meeting death ready and at peace, with the satisfaction of a life fully lived.

Fear of death is one of the great afflictions of our time. We are no longer able to accept death as the natural conclusion of our experience in the world, and to welcome it with serenity. Society in the western world tries to convince us that dying is the worst evil, but it's not true: living badly is the worst evil. Together with dying in fear and with no awareness. All of life is a preparation for dying, through the happy moments as well as the challenges and pain.

In these stories, the protagonists' life ends when they have completed their mission, and they are aware of it. Death is then truly just a Passage to a new journey, a new life. The most precious moment to make sense of it all.

The lives in this collection are anchors in time, an embroidery of points of presence drawing a map for anyone who gets excited discovering them. In this way, the lives themselves become more real as events turn into myths, just like in the tales of heroes' deeds.

What, indeed, makes a life real after it has ended? That its events are recounted and the story resonates again, in words and rhythms, pauses and images. Not just memories destined to vanish, but new emotions that enrich, complete and change the way of being of those listening to them. This is also a way not to be afraid of death, and to make the essence of our presence in this world eternal. Life after life we are timeless, precisely through the experience of our mortality.

1.5 How did I Find These Stories?

These tales are the result of my investigations along the lines of time, through a method I learned at Damanhur.

Damanhur—founded by a group of spiritual seekers in the early 1970s—is a community dedicated to discovering the deeper meanings of life through art, spirituality, and an ever-increasing awareness of human nature and our role in the universe. The cosmos, in Damanhurian philosophy, is a conscious entity, evolving together with the planets and the stars, and every particle of consciousness, including the individual one of each human being.

My training began first with teaching and then also researching individual and collective adventures on the paths of time. At Damanhur we have developed an accurate system of investigation, validated by the memories of thousands of people around the world who follow this method to become more aware of their presence at various points in time.

The process involves several steps, in special places and moments. It starts by tuning into the aura of the person whose lives are being sought, through a photograph, their name and birth data. They represent both the frequency of that person within the current flow of time, as well as their authorization to follow their temporal tracks and meet the lives most useful for their growth at that moment. The same research, conducted for example ten years later, could lead to different results, if the spiritual state of the person requesting the investigation is different: the doors of time open by vibrational correspondence with your spiritual alignment, revealing what's most useful for your evolution, whether it's healing from trauma or recovering talents and possibilities.

In this age of Awakening—in which so many are reclaiming their psychic abilities and following profound spiritual yearnings—it's certainly possible for you to retrieve your memories on your own—perhaps with a little guidance by someone with experience, to make it easier and more direct. Indeed, it's an excellent starting point to become familiar with time as a territory in which you can move. I actually devote most of my teaching to this. However, a life "found" for us, as the result of a ritualized research—and free of those expectations and judgments which often influence the way we see ourselves—if it's well written can become an artistic creation, and be a true gift.

I've seen the events I tell in these stories as if I were there, or felt their vividness within me; at other times, I've observed them from the outside and then written them down. Sometimes, it was as if the story was being dictated to me: in re-reading it, I met the protagonist for the first time. To make the tales more engaging and understandable for this book, I added some details and a few more elements about the thoughts and feelings of the person telling their story. Some characters like to talk about themselves in depth, others prefer to convey their lives in pictures or flashes of feeling.

The stories of each of these lives have been shared with the person who requested the research. As the memories resurfaced, in their body, heart and mind, the story became more vivid and more present. Indeed, for every life I've documented, the most valuable treasure is in the emotions and memories of those who relive it, making it more "real" along the timeline. Now, your own feelings upon hearing or reading them, create yet another layer of reality on each of these existences.

The great psychoanalyst Karl Gustav Jung wrote in the Red Book, published posthumously in 2009: "*For the sake of truth I must tell you that I belong neither to this time nor to this place. For many years a spell has confined me to this place and time. In reality I am not the one you see before you.*"

Jung was convinced that reincarnation originated from the memories of the collective unconscious. In accordance with his thinking, my decades of research indicate that all memories are contained in a reservoir of collective energy and information, and memories of a life lived by one person can, by correspondence and affinity, awaken those of another. These stories have the potential to help you, too, who read or listen to them, activate your memories and make your presence more real within the fabric of time.

1.6 Reading Tips

These are not conventional tales: the words capture the essence of an entire life, focusing on key moments. Let your feelings and thoughts transport you, as you read or listen to these stories.

If you read or listen to them before sleeping, let them guide your dreams.

Open your heart and imagine you're taking off to discover new possibilities, and ignite sparks of your deepest memories. Your "here and now" has strong connections to other points in time that, though past compared to your today, are all other "here and now's" for your essence.

Let the stories take you on a journey of imagination, as your sensations fill in the details, so that every experience can become fully yours, too. Probably, you know about them more than you may imagine at first, and as you share the joys and challenges of these characters, your awareness of the meaning of your own life, your choices, and your relationships with others may deepen, too.

Summon up a feeling of gentleness and connection to life in your heart. It's a spiritual practice, and a way for your brain to become more activated and your mind more expanded. Indeed, loving kindness and compassion strengthen gamma waves—the fastest brain frequency with the smallest amplitude, which instantly connect information in every part of the brain—creating a coherent and unified perception.

Strong in this inner alchemy of love and intelligence, you can cultivate your trust in the existence of a greater plan than you can see. You are within an infinite flow of Consciousness and can, in every moment, choose to follow it: that is the direction, the north of your compass.

We've been born and reborn countless times,
and it's possible that every being
was our parent in one life or another.
Therefore, it is plausible that all beings
in this universe have ties of kinship.

His Holiness the Sixteenth Dalai Lama

ONCE UPON A TIME THERE WAS...

A MAN WHO DIDN'T RETURN TO THE STARS

Lush forests in Central America. Very ancient times.

I was born here, but we are not from here. Our ancestors came with a ship from the stars: it crashed in this forest. There is still a part of its structure we can enter. It used to be the command center of this vessel, now it's the sacred place where we can still contact the cosmic forces we are connected to. There we hear their voices; from there they still guide us. Their instructions are clear: we have to establish their presence here, create a link from the worlds they preside over, to this new one. There is no hope of going back.

Nothing on this planet was familiar to the first ones who arrived here. It is so far from everything, so different from our original home-world. I know this from the stories the elders tell us, but I am the third generation, I feel my homeland is here! Our fathers and mothers still looked up at the sky with longing. They felt it was their direction home.

We feel the stars were just our point of departure. The elders say we are the ones that will make the great transitions, we are their hope for the future. We are on this planet to stay, and we will shape this world in a new way.

Our genetic transformation is guided and planned from the sacred space of the Ship, and it's a success! We have in us the energetic matrix of this planet mixed with the original one of our people; our bodies already show physical signs of adaptation to the new environment. We can eat many more foods than our parents can; we can live outdoors; our bodies know how to follow the rhythms of the day and the night, that have almost the same length.

We are all connected, but the impulses that guide us do not come from the ship anymore, as it was for our ancestors. We are freer, more independent. I love the sense of having a space in my mind all for myself, in which I can create anything I want. I can make choices according to many more variables than the ones the original group-mind allowed. It's exhilarating! I have a strong imagination and a sense of adventure that I want to cultivate in every possible way.

I'm tall and graceful like all of us. I want to fully enjoy my body and my senses, on this fragrant land.

We soon discover that more separation in our minds increases intimacy, and extends the range of pleasures our body gives us. Touching, smelling, making love and sharing physical space with our new, well defined mental boundaries is a constant discovery for us! A fascinating, and amusing, field of research.

We live in beautiful stone dwellings, carved with exquisite grace by the humans who live in this area, according to the mental instructions we give them. This land is rich in precious stones, and we use them to give shape and direction to the energetic flows of the space around us. The local people who work for us are small and docile, it's very easy to guide their minds and their actions. We are grateful to them, we keep them healthy and youthful with our healing energy fields. They remember very little of the work they do for us, nor do they recall where we live. It all has the flavor of a dream for them.

They think we are gods that descended from the heavens. And like gods, we manifest at specific times of the year, when we open the energetic bubble that separates our area in the forest from the rest of the land. On those occasions, we let the local people see some of us to inspire awe. I gladly do this, whenever I can. I like to cross the barrier and walk in the "other world," feeling the waves of emotions of all those people assembled to honor us.

We need to start creating our own civilization on this planet, and building a city is part of my group's task. It grows fast thanks to our technology and the relentless work of our human workers. It is harmonious, full of water and palaces, terraces and temples. It will become a splendid home for us and our future descendants.

My body doesn't last as long as expected. The genetic transformation has made us more earthly, but our life span has conspicuously decreased. Our scientists take all my life parameters to study them, and create a more resilient future generation. I know I'll come back in one of the new bodies.

When the geneticists are finished, I lay in one of the Chairs of Passage on the ship. I let my spirit unite to my ancestors in the stars, within the protected energetic area created by our gods, beyond all space and time. Only then, I fully comprehend the greatness of their plan.

I can see down the timelines of so many generations: there is a new path of evolution that will lead to a new world, so distant in the future to be just a small light.

A radiance far, far away, but invincible with the essence of a new power called "Love." I understand this is the way to regain the complete connection my people originally had, while maintaining the freedom of mind that has made me so happy in this life.

A sacred merging of communion and individuality, to create a new, luminous Human Soul in the heart of the universe.

A PRINCESS WHO SOUGHT THE ABSOLUTE

Ancient Mesopotamia. Age of maximum splendor of the Sumerian Empire.

The greatness of my people is written in the stars.

I've known this since I was a child, and I'd walk with my father, at night, along the banks of the great river. I was his favorite daughter, among the many he had fathered. Perhaps because, like him, I loved spending time in silence contemplating the sky, feeling that special bond between us.

I realize at a young age that I don't see the world as others do. I am not like other people. My eyes see beyond physical forms, and my senses perceive patterns, relationships, attractions and oppositions. In my mind everything is broken down to its basic components, and then re-assembled on many possible lines of probability and existence.

My father can't deny me anything, so he doesn't object to my studies, even though they were normally reserved to men. The priests disagree, but he scoffs at them, saying he has enough daughters to marry off for all the necessary alliances. And knowledge knows no gender, it just wants a brilliant mind, much passion and dedication.

I learn several languages quickly; each has a different logic, each is a key to a part of my mind. Mathematics is my passion: in the harmony of complex calculations I see the power of the gods, I feel their thoughts, I intuit their plans. This is what I'll dedicate my life to: I want to transcend this plane of existence, find the secret of the universe and our role in it.

Our kingdom is powerful and our culture refined: its many pleasures are known from across the sea. Everyone wants to experience them, also the best tutors in the world. They gladly teach me and other students, while enjoying the sweetness of our eternal spring. I love my land deeply; nothing can demonstrate the benevolence of the gods for humankind more than its beauty, its scents, and its colors. Our great sacred rivers are tears of the gods, fallen on Earth to bring us prosperity and life.

I study the sky, spending night after night watching the movements of the stars and planets. I have the most sophisticated equipment there is, protected by armed guards. No one can touch it. My living quarters are full of scrolls, books and maps, but I spend most of my time on my big terrace where a lush garden, full of plants and flowers attracts wonderful butterflies and birds that sing happily to the sky.

I especially love the scent of jasmine flowers, I feel it sharpens my mind.

Music helps me open my senses and my perceptions. I grasp its harmony, and listening to it often opens avenues in my understanding. I have a group of musicians who play just for me, trained to take me to a state of lucid trance, where my thoughts have no limits.

I spend long periods alone, totally absorbed in my studies and then, suddenly, another me surfaces for a while. It's an urge to feel my body, the energy of life coursing through my veins. I summon sweet, strong and beautiful lovers, or I fight for fun with the royal instructors who trained me as a child. Sometimes this state of exaltation and connection to my body lasts only a few hours, sometimes a few days. Then I immerse myself with even more concentration in my studies.

I know the stars are alive; they have meaning and a voice. I hear their calling, and I write down everything they tell me. They reveal to me how they pull the strings of destiny, acknowledging and respecting the choices of humans. There is perfection and balance, and an eternal wisdom. Time is the essence of it. And there is a Design in time for all of us. Here and now, and at so many other points. Every life a point, every life an extension of a signal that comes from afar.

I understand when all the data I needed to collect are complete. My time in this body is over; the project entrusted to me is concluded. Now I can rejoin the totality, the universe, the gods.

It's a beautiful starry night, the jasmine is in full bloom. I smell its sweet scent, while the musicians play my favorite melody. Slowly, I drink the potion that will take my soul to the stars. I am aware and ready.

A FOREST OF SACRED OAKS

Celtic people in central Europe.

I was born on a summer morning, and my people say I carry the sweet warmth of that moment wherever I go. My people are kind and loving. Not so much through words, because we don't talk much, but through gestures and, even more so, through our thoughts. We feel the ideas of others as if they were a wave of energy on our skin. That's why, already as children, we learn the right formulas and proper breathing to guide our emotions and control our minds. Sharing out-of-balance feelings and bad thoughts with others is unacceptable behavior because it spreads malaise to everyone.

We live deep in the forest, and she is our Mother. We have many rituals to honor the Great Tree that regulates and harmonizes the lives of all beings in the forest. Among my people, it's the old priestess who listens to the voice of that oak tree and transmits to us the will and decisions of Spirit. She has spent so much time near the Tree that she now resembles it. Her skin is brown and wrinkled, her body moves very slowly, and her eyes are as green as leaves. They say that's why she was chosen: priestesses are all born with green eyes.

There's a girl like that in my village, she arrived among us a few seasons after me. Already as a child I feel a special bond with her, an instinct to protect her, and a desire to be with her as much as possible. We grow up playing together, exploring the forest together, learning the myths and songs of our people. Near her, I feel happy and complete. My heart sings to the sky and the sun during the day, and to the stars at night. Most of all, my chest is filled with a warm and powerful feeling for her. It's the gentle touch of her thoughts on my skin that makes me feel strong and joyful.

We've grown up now, I want to be with her completely, sleep with her under our trees, see her eyes in the morning when I wake up. The Elders give us their permission, but they warn us that the day will come when she'll be called to take the place of the Priestess at the Sacred Oak. We must accept this condition. I don't mind too much, we're still so young, we have so much time ahead of us. And maybe another girl with eyes like leaves will be born to our people, so that my beloved will never have to leave me.

I know the forest well and I sense where it hides its treasures. I go in search of berries and mushrooms, bark and moss for food and medicine.

I collect wood and sometimes participate in the rituals of felling a tree. We very rarely do this, we prefer to live in natural caves rather than end the lives of living trees, but sometimes it is necessary. We prepare offerings to the Spirit of the Tree, paint ritual marks on our faces with clay and ashes, and ask the tree to share its experience with the other trees, so that only its body is sacrificed.

It's after one of these rituals that, upon returning home, I find our dwelling empty. I realize that the time has come for my woman to become the Voice of the Tree. I use all the techniques I have learned, but the pain I feel in my heart cannot be appeased. I leave the village because I don't want to contaminate others with my out-of-control emotions.

I wander in the forest for a long time. I see the color of the leaves change, the waters become darker and colder. For the first time in my life I feel a horrible sense of being truly alone, locked within the confines of my body and my suffering. Where is the touch of everyone else's presence? Where are the whispers of the trees and all the animals in the forest? Where are the voices of Fire and Air, and that of Water? Why does the earth beneath my feet not guide my steps?

I don't know how much time has passed, but little by little the storm of my emotions calms down, and I begin to perceive the forest answering my questions. I feel as if it's speaking in the voice of my beloved. It helps me understand the value of her sacrifice and mine, the importance of her mission for all of us...

I roam for some more time, then I finally feel that everything inside me finds a new order. I realize that being able to keep her close to me for so long has been a great gift. Now, I must understand what my role is for my people. I decide that I too will serve the Tree. In this way, the connection with my beloved will remain alive and at a higher level, in service to the well-being of all. I realize that the energy that our love and union have created is not only a gift to us, but, more importantly, to our people.

Back at the village I'm welcomed with gentle, tender touches of affection and friendship from everyone. I see my beloved from a distance, and feel there's a different presence in her. The old Priestess is dying, and her powers are being transferred to the one taking her place.

I shave my head, and wear a simple tunic. I join the Servants of the Oak.

Our role is to keep the physical and spiritual space around the Tree clean and pure. We help people who come with questions to prepare for their encounter with the profound wisdom of the Mother Tree.

I'm once again close to the woman I love and, once again, protecting her is part of my duties. With a sense of awe and gratitude I see her transforming more and more, becoming a strong and clean channel of communication with the Ancestors and the spirit world.

Like everyone in my people, I sense when the time of my death is approaching. I see a bite mark on my foot and understand that the Powers of the Beyond have chosen a small being of the forest to come calling for me.

The poison takes a day to draw my spirit out of my body. I feel the Tree opening the passage for me. Its strong presence mixes with the sweet sensation of the essence of the Priestess, my great love, guiding me to the other side.

A GEISHA WHO FOUND PERFECTION

Feudal Japan.

I know every secret of my body. Every cell, every tiniest part of my skin responds to my commands. I have tamed my body with my mind; my mind with my will, and my will with Beauty.

Beauty is the most severe teacher, the one who demands the most extreme discipline. It can gift you with the absolute, but in return it asks for a complete surrender. I learned this as a child. My parents' house is a pristine container of harmony. Nothing must disturb the perfection my father demands, and my mother creates. Even the distance between two stems of flowers is calculated. Everything is related, everything is in balance, objects define the space. Everything must be placed according to a hierarchy that recreates the order of the universe, and gives the feeling that time and its effects cannot reach us.

Rarely do we speak at home. Sound has a power to be directed through prayer or song. Sound sculpts space. I learn to sing as soon as I have control of my voice; then I learn to play a stringed instrument, and finally a flute. My father summons teachers for me when I'm still a child. I dance, draw, study philosophy, and compose poetry.

I learn the secret language of flowers and colors. I have my father's quick mind and the extraordinary beauty of my mother. I am taught to find meaning in everything. Every moment of my life has a purpose.

When I reach the appropriate age, I move to the School with some other girls. I must excel in all the arts to become a valuable asset to my father. Not the wife of a single man, but maybe the muse and confidante of a few of the most powerful men in the country.

The place is beautiful. I love the house we live in, it's full of artworks, and it's much more colorful than my parents' home. The garden is magnificent; we spend plenty of time taking care of the flowers, contemplating their beauty, understanding their language. They have a power that influences moods and feelings. Our teachers pass on to us the ancient secrets of all the arts: music subdues the mind; poetry enchants the heart; dance ignites it. Discipline sometimes creates pain; pain becomes pleasure, and pleasure opens the doors of transcendence.

I undergo many initiations. Every time, a part of me must die so that I can be renewed, stronger, more aware. Many prayer-formulas, practices, rituals.

The search for perfection and the suffering to reach it are my most constant companions. Several years go by, demanding and testing and yet suspended in time, like a deep breath. I know how to guide my mind and my heart, I've learned a thousand ways to create harmony with music, with conversations, with the movements of my body, and with the play of folding fans. I've learned to feed on the energies of the night, and rest during the day. I'm a work of art creating pure Beauty.

I prepare for my first official appearance with great care. As the makeup transforms my face, I feel the powers I've gained complete me, layer by layer. Just as the layers of fabric of my robes create a sort of armor of energy, the container for the emotions I need to arouse and direct. Like the other women who have completed their training, I am now an activator of male power. Without us there would be no princes, no warriors, no emperors. Without us the masculine principle would not dwell in the souls and bodies of men. There would be no harmony, no life. Only chaos and ignorance.

I am ready to embrace my new Name, the frequency that represents my power. When I hear it pronounced for the first time, announcing my presence in the House, I feel my heart beat faster. I sense the amazement and admiration of the nobles who are there, when they feel the power of the Gift I bring. I sing, dance, answer riddles, and debate philosophical matters with graceful poetry. I serve tea, food and drinks, feeling the eternal play of energies between the masculine and feminine principles capturing us in its ancient dance.

The noblest of the guests requests that I be exclusively for him. The amount he offers cannot be refused. The young woman inside me quivers with pleasure at his first touch, but my training connects me to something so ancient that I quickly regain control of my emotions. Behind my contained expression, I feel so much happiness that my heart has also accepted the request to be the Muse of this man. I want to explore myself to the fullest, I feel it will be easier if I focus my energies with just one patron.

I choose to live with some of my sisters. We have great respect for each other, and don't need to talk much. It's a life of beauty, intense dedication, and constant refinement. The quest for perfection is my spiritual path. I'm never alone in walking it: the ancient voices of all those before me whisper in my ear. For many seasons the cherry trees bloom, and then lose their flowers. I learn to open deep doors in the man I serve and inspire: visions and insights for the future, for governance, for war strategies.

He sees his own death on the battlefield, and together we prepare for it. When it actually happens I feel it in my body. It's a painful tear, but then the unbearable silence of his absence gives way to the understanding that life is an unstoppable flow: it was, it is, it will be. Just like the cherry blossoms.

I am now rich and powerful. I've learned everything I needed to, and now I can teach. I am entrusted with many girls. I guide them with discipline and silent love for many seasons. I nurture the precious seed of Beauty contained within them until it becomes a strong and majestic tree, a connection to unite the world of humans to that of the gods.

I die serene, ready, on my tatami. The melodious singing of my favorite student accompanies me. She's not allowed to cry, I don't want any disharmony to mar her exquisite voice.

A POET IN ATLANTIS CREATING REALITY

Golden Age of Atlantis. About 23,000 years ago.

All the records of our history are kept in the archives of my Family, from the time when our ancestors left one of the central planets in the galaxy and arrived here, where we are today, in the heart of the most splendid civilization humans have ever created.

Millennia have passed since the first arrival, but we are still recognizable by our long necks and the different shape of the front of our skulls. Our brains have more developed layers than most of the races that, like us, live on the central continent. From this come the psychic faculties that we all have in our Family.

We are one of the oldest and noblest Families, and for us, nobility has two meanings: Service and Harmony. Many of us are legislators, royal advisors, consultants for great architectural works, musicians and poets. We are present whenever a higher order needs to be comprehended and advocated.

Unlike other clans, in ours, men and women have the same opportunities, and the traits of the two genders are not always clearly distinguishable.

This is a gift left by the original androgyny of our ancestors. In us, the masculine and feminine principles are both awakened and integrated. Sexual orientation is a choice, not a destiny determined by genes.

I was born in an area of beautiful gardens, close to the Capital; that's where I grew up. We also own a palace in the inner circle, where we hold family gatherings during the great annual celebrations. Since my childhood, I've had access to the great temples where I am introduced to the Ancient Forces presiding over the proper unfolding of my life and mission.

I'm very sensitive and I experience a wider range of feelings than average. Due to genetic predisposition and our role, all members of my Family are allowed this amplitude of sensations by law. It has long been understood that well guided emotions shape reality in a positive way, but when they are out of balance they become powerful weapons, also against oneself. For this reason, in our harmonious civilization, only a few Guilds can experience the full range of sensations—human and not only. Some Guilds can also perceive the feelings of other beings and races, but only if this ability is in service to the growth of all.

My training is devoted to all the arts, to the study of the history and customs, languages, social and physical structures of all the peoples of Atlantis, and beyond. To serve Harmony, it is necessary to understand the richness of diversity, divest oneself of all judgment, and seek the purity of Essence. My life is dedicated to this task, and I'm proud of it.

After completing my training, during my Ritual of Ignition, I wear the indigo silk robe indicating my caste and role: from that moment I feel One with the life stream guiding our people to its final actualization.

I choose the role of Poet. This is an extremely important function, because a Poet writes, and therefore creates, History through Beauty that becomes Truth. Not only do I recount what happened, but I add emotional layers on top of each story to make it more real, and therefore visible also to the gods. It is these Forces that validate all events at the end of time, making our plane of reality true.

We Poets are the link between human vicissitudes and the dimension where events become real: our attention increases the complexity of what we choose to include in the story of our time, so that occurrences are oriented in the right direction.

This is how the complex living system of the universe works: by saturating events with refined emotions and harmony, we guide our people towards an enlightened future.

I perform many hours of practice in the arts of movement, breathing and meditation. I often spend time in the gardens observing plants and especially insects. Their orbits hide universal secrets and patterns.

I choose my every gesture, I select carefully every type of food and drink, every contact. My body is my laboratory. Through a correct relationship with my cells, I can arouse and distill in me the emotions I then transform into poetry. It takes courage to embrace everything; love to ignite my heart—the engine for my emotions—and detachment to feel without influencing. The Word is the ultimate receptacle of my process of participation in Life.

The masculine and feminine sides are both active in me; they mix and alternate with emotional waves to guide me. In order to nourish the primeval power of the androgynous Being within me, I have love relationships with men and women. They all belong to my Family as the different frequency of any other human would contaminate my energy reservoir, and affect my health, too.

I deposit all my work at the House of History, through an ancient ritual that transforms poetic sounds into Words of Power to summon the attention of Higher Forces. Every gesture has its rightful place, everything is part of a great spiritual device that will lead all of us to higher and higher levels of knowledge and wisdom. I have no doubt about this.

I live a long life, and carefully plan my return. I choose to reincarnate within the same Family, and record my memories in the Central Crystal of Atlantis. A part of me also remains in the crystal at the Family palace, where all the lives of my lineage are intertwined. Scientists prepare emotional and hormonal essences to give to my next me to accelerate the awakening of memories.

I leave my body at the chosen time in the Family Palace. There is a great light around me: I become the Harmony I've always served.

A NOBLEWOMAN WHO LOVED A PRIEST, AND MARRIED A MERCHANT

Italy. Rome. 16th century.

This palace is my protection and my cage. I am the third child of one of the most important Roman families, the only daughter. Many of my ancestors were bishops, so we are closely related to the papacy. Around me there is beauty and opulence in everything, in every room of the palace, every object, piece of furniture, dress, type of food... but unfortunately not in the people.

Since I was a child, I've had the strange characteristic of sensing with my skin, as if there were messages coming from the air, going through my body. I feel them inside me. I often cry as a child, I'm often scared and I don't know why. As I grow up, I learn to contain my emotions and smile, but I still perceive the traces of the thoughts and feelings my father, my brothers and their many guests leave in the building. They are never pleasant.

I'm being raised to become a bargaining chip, and one day increase my family's power. My father is very pleased with my beauty; he says it makes me worth more. As soon as I become a girl, he assigns me a personal maid to take care of my most important asset.

She styles my hair, chooses my clothes, and later trains me on how to please a man. It takes me years to realize that this woman is my father's mistress, and I am her gateway to living in the palace.

She prepares me and, more importantly, controls me, selecting what I can read and listen to, restricting where I can go, and whom I can see. I have to shut off all emotions, but the effort is too great and I fall ill with a strange disease. I have no strength left; I no longer eat; I spend more time in the strange world of dreams than in the reality around me. This illness is my salvation.

My father summons a priest to stay close to me, and prepare me in case I were to die. He is kind and elegant in his manners and speech, well educated and about my father's age. For the first time in my life, I feel a light coming from a human being, and trails of emotions that reassure me, comfort me. For the first time, I am not afraid. For the first time, I don't feel lonely.

Conversations with the priest restore my will to live. It takes many months, but little by little I open my heart and mind. For the first time, I feel the presence of my soul, a Light reaching me from far away, stronger than any sad or dark feeling coming from men: it's a feeling that overwhelms me, mixed with an attraction, a confusion, an unknown flow of energy. It makes me feel connected to the priest as if he were a part of me. I feel life flowing through me like never before. I spend every moment preparing for our meetings and conversations, which, since I've been feeling better, take place in the garden, amidst the scent of flowers and the gentle sound of the water flowing in the fountains.

Not only does my body heal, so does my soul. I am stronger, more present, no longer afraid. And it's only thanks to this transformation that I can face the most difficult period of my life. The priest is sent away all of a sudden, and then my father announces the date of my wedding. I'm healthy now, and he doesn't want to waste time and risk me having more crises: my marriage with a rich merchant will fill the family coffers, as my father will obtain a percentage of a thriving spice and silk trade. Finally, my father tells me coldly, I've become the precious asset he invested so much in perfecting.

I meet my groom a few days before the wedding. His face and arms are covered with scars, he looks more like a pirate than a merchant. The trail he leaves is dark and opaque, but I feel I need not fear him. Indeed, I soon discover that his interest in me doesn't extend beyond his agreement with my father, guaranteeing him the rights to new routes.

Immediately after the wedding, I move to his palace. It's less luxurious than my father's, but I am much freer. I rarely see him, he never touches me.

I devote myself to my studies; I hire new teachers and start writing, especially philosophical and religious reflections. My faith grows stronger, and I find comfort praying in a monastery in the countryside, where I go every day. I dream that one day I'll meet the priest again, but all my attempts to find him fail. I direct the river of emotions in my heart to God, and little by little I find peace.

My husband dies ten years after our wedding, in a clash with bandits in the East. I don't hesitate for a moment. I give all my property to the monastery, and ask to be admitted as a novice. When I see my long, cropped hair falling at my feet, a feeling of freedom fills my heart. I spend many years in prayer and service at the monastery. I continue to contemplate and write. No frightening feelings reach me inside these walls; every trail of emotion is purified by the Grace of God.

I die when I am forty years old, while I'm praying. I am ready, death announced itself, and I was waiting. Leaving my body is a great relief. I follow a trail of light and feel completely free.

A BLIND WIZARD RIDING IN THE STEPPE

Twelfth century. Great plains of Asia.
Army of Genghis Khan.

There are no veils I didn't cross. I've fought and thrown myself into territories where no one before me dared to walk. I've glimpsed the greatness of the human spirit, and encountered the basest of instincts. I've smelled blood and fear, and the ineffable scent of the heavens, after the spirits quieted and came to me.

I worked hard to acquire this power; my life is completely dedicated to it, the rhythms of my breath are the same of the cosmos. I feel them in me. It has always been this way, ever since I was a child. A special child—this was clear even before I was born. My mother had strange dreams, and I remember them all. I could feel the world waiting for me before I was born into it.

When my soul awakened, in my early teens, the memories came back and I knew who I was. It was the gods who chose me, and then chose for me. I cannot see with my physical eyes, but I perceive much more than anyone else. People are shapes of energy and color; I've learned to penetrate them, change their vibration, transform thoughts and feelings.

I can make men invincible, or make them flee in terror. I'm one of the most powerful weapons in our invincible army.

I know the Khan fears me too, I perceive the light of the amulet he wears to protect himself from me. He does not need it, my loyalty to him is unfaltering. And so is my love for him. I forgive him for this small weakness; I pretend not to feel that gleam, which I could obscure with a single breath.

None of his magicians are as powerful as I am. It is I who call the Spirits of Battle. I'm the one leading them so that they ride with our army, swift and unstoppable as the wind of steppe. I can fly with them, be close to my Khan, make him invincible. I know the herbs, mushrooms and roots of our land, and how to combine them to open all the Gates, sustain my strength, and move my consciousness as far as it needs to go.

My yurt is comfortable; there are many furs that connect me to the power of animals. I wear precious clothes, fur coats, amulets and jewelry with magical powers. I inspire a feeling of awe. I am tall and strong; with my long hair I hear the voice of the wind. Mine is the power of Air, my element. A sparrow hawk sits on my shoulder—the only being that can enter my tent at will: he brings me messages, he's my voice to his brothers in the sky and to the Powers of the High. We are both free, and I respect him for that.

I know the pleasures of life, and I welcome them when necessary: food, drink and sex are tools I balance with intention to nourish my energy field, and create a living alchemy of forces to offer the Spirits. I let skilled and gentle hands massage my body with scented oils; precious woods and resins always burn in my tent to sustain the power of my inner sight.

I ride as fast as the best of our knights; I precede the army onto the field before each battle to prepare for victory, and invoke the spirits of nature so that they are on our side. I often have to fight on the astral planes before the army even deploys. I have hordes of demons at my service. Our gods are the most powerful, and we know what offerings they demand, what is well received by them. Our priests worship and pray; they make ritual sacrifices, and the spells of our enemies melt away like snow in the sun.

I'm also the last to walk on the battlefield after the fight is over. I direct the spirits of our brave warriors to the House of the Beyond; I ask the demons of death to be merciful, and give them a fair reward for the sacrifice of their lives. None of our people walk alone to the Beyond.

I love this life of constant exploration, of ceaseless movement. March after march, battle after battle, we carry the greatness of our people and our gods farther and farther. We conquer the world to bring a new civilization, a new order, to create one great, united people.

I know my time is over the night my sparrow-hawk doesn't return. In his place a raven enters my tent. I'm not afraid. I wear my most beautiful clothes, dressing slowly and with great care, then I walk to the top of the hill. I sense the camp fires and the Khan's tent down below. I know that tomorrow will bring a great victory.

I smile as I feel the wind carry my spirit out of my body. I hear the thud of my physical vessel falling on the ground. Snow quickly covers it, as the Gates of the Beyond open before me. I am not alone on the Path.

A MEDIUM WHO DANCED TO THE MOON

Brazil. Bahia. Sixteenth century.

I was born with music in my blood, that's what everyone tells me, laughing. They say I was already dancing in the cradle, and my first cry was as melodious as a song. It's a happy village where my mother lives; she's young, and very beautiful in my eyes. She has the fairest skin of all: the villagers tell my grandmother's story with a touch of irreverence mixed with admiration. They say she had the courage to follow her heart, and then chose to return to her people, bringing with her a child so fair-skinned that the moon seemed to have kissed her at birth.

At the village, there's laughter, chatter and singing in the air at all times, for every occasion we have a song. I can't imagine how I could live without each and every one of these people: we're like one big family. The forest welcomes and protects us, we respect and venerate its forces and spirits.

In the air, the scent of the ocean mingles with that of the trees. We reach it very quickly, sailing in small canoes on the river through the jungle until we get to a white beach and an immense expanse of blue light. I love the ocean so much! I enjoy swimming underwater following the sparkle of the sun's rays on the surface.

I grow up strong and healthy because on every occasion I immerse myself in its waters. I know it's the home of a very powerful and ancient spirit, and I always feel welcomed by it.

Our men go fishing, and collect precious shells and other wonders from the sea; we women gather fruits from the trees and prepare food and bread. Sometimes some of us go as far as the big village where the light-skinned men live, but the stories they tell us when they get back are not pretty. I have no interest in going there, there's so much to explore right here where I am!

My body moves all the time, following a rhythm I feel inside me. It gives me so much energy and joy. I feel it's the leaves in the trees, the clouds in the sky, the waves in the ocean moving through me. I think it's their way of communicating with us, but I can't understand what they are saying. I talk to the elders about it and they tell me that maybe I have a precious gift for everyone, but I have to wait until I get older—then we'll see.

I continue my life with joy in my heart. I have many friends, also among the animals, especially the birds singing to the sky at the first glow of day and the monkeys screaming loudly in response to my voice.

When I become a woman, and my blood flows to the rhythm of the moon, the older wise woman tells me it's time to give my gift a try. During the ceremonies around the fire I'm allowed to join the central circle. I drink a strong bitter liquid, then the head medium invites me to dance with her and the others. At the sound of the drums, the rhythm inside me turns into a roar; I feel myself enveloped by a strong light and then I see the circle of dancers from above. My body moves with new movements, with an energy I've never felt before. I fly over the village for a while, then I lose all perceptions.

When I wake up in my hut, it's already almost evening. I feel dizzy but I have a new sensation in my heart, the light touch of an ancient and wise power. Since that time, at every full moon, the spirits called by the head medium enter my body and bring messages for my people—sometimes they heal us, sometimes they warn us. I am so happy to be of service!

My life is full of gifts. One of the most beautiful is the strong and brave man, who makes my heart beat. He's one of the most skilled fishermen; with his canoe he's the fastest of all and always brings me presents from the sea. The most precious gifts are our children: I love and protect them, and then I do the same with their children.

The village of the white people expands and they venture deeper into the forest; our sentinels spot them more and more often. My instincts tell me this is not a good thing. Many of us are leaving, looking for a different life closer to the whites. We're worried and curious about what fate holds for them, but they never come back to tell us. The spirits warn us about dangers and death. I don't know what awaits my people, but even with worry in my heart I smile and sing, to share the joy of my life with all.

I leave my body after a challenging ceremony; the light I know welcomes me, and I hear the whispers of the Forces pointing me clearly in one direction amidst many different paths. I'm not old, but all the energy I've devoted to being a channel has consumed me. I don't regret a single moment of my life, not a single choice.

A MAN ON THE PATHS OF DREAM AND SOUND

Northern Australia. Ancient times.

The drum of life beats in unison with the rhythm of my heart. With each pulsation creation repeats itself, keeping the world around me solid. With each pause everything fades away and the space of silent sound opens up, where I can travel without my legs, without my eyes, without my hands. When the sound is suspended, the door to enter another world appears. Since I was a child I've learned to control the beating of my heart, slowing it down, to open a wider passage, easier to cross.

At first it's just a game, a challenge with the other kids. I'm taller than they, and stronger. My father and my grandfather, and his father's father also had exceptional strength. They could walk longer than the others; they could run and hunt with more strength, and they performed many brave acts for the sake of our people. I don't want to be any less.

I love my body; I like to perceive it from the inside, feeling its strength and the matter of which it is made, that is as old as the earth and the ashes with which I cover and decorate it. My breath is so powerful that my people say I could be the son of the blowing wind.

I laugh, but I feel that it's indeed something special, a gift of life: I must understand how to use it for the good of all. Only in this way will the gods be happy. Only in this way will I have my rightful place as a Man among Men. This is the most important value: our life is made sacred, at every heartbeat, by our being one with each other, with the sky, the earth, animals, plants and rocks.

Sound is the most powerful force, the most sacred medicine. Sound opens all doors, even those of the heart. My first solo journey is to find my own sound. My quest follows a trail I feel with my skin. I walk on paths of dirt and rock I touch with my feet, and other bright and variable trails that I follow without carrying my weight. There, I hear the voices of the ancestors: in this space they've created waves of shapes and colors. It's like a mirror world, more alive and more colorful, stitched together by constant streams of light energy and emotions. I don't carry my body with me, yet I can see, feel, direct my movements.

Every time I return to the solid world, and touch with my hands my gradually awakening body, I feel a joy so deep I can hardly contain it. We are the People of Men, we walk in the garden with our tree and animal brothers and sisters, and with them we go through the gates of the great rivers of light.

We have another life there; with each new passage we weave threads connecting us, creating a path that is ever more solid and easier to find. Until the gods return, and together with them we'll give birth to another world, with no more suffering or death.

I hear my tree calling to me, but it takes me several dawns to find it. When I finally meet it, I feel a deep emotion. A sudden tiredness seizes me: I know I must not resist it. I lay down under the large eucalyptus tree, and breathe to slow my heart. I immediately feel myself being pulled down, faster and faster, until my perception overlaps with the roots of the tree. It's there that I hear for the first time the sound I am to create. That will be my sound, the vibration it's my duty to add to the voices of my people. I feel it in my every cell, and for the first time I know what it means to be truly alive, welcomed by the community of Life itself.

When I awaken, I immediately see the large, hollowed branch assigned to me: the father-tree has accepted me, I have his trust, and I can take a piece of him to become part of me. I return to the village, and thanks to the patient guidance of an elder, I prepare my instrument during many seasons. Every transformation of the wood takes place within me. I am each termite that hollowed it out; I dry up parts that are longer needed in me; it's my spirit I'm molding as I create the mouthpiece with pure wax, a gift from our sisters the bees. It's me tuning into the rhythm of the universe to be the right sound.

I undergo several initiations and new trials, while awake or in the dream-world, until I truly become a man. When my preparation ends I can choose my role. I want to heal my people. I hardly speak anymore, so as not to contaminate the sound with unnecessary emissions. I must concentrate the sacred power of rhythm in every way.

Sometimes I heal individuals, but these are exceptions in really serious cases. I take care of the whole village, together, on the plane where we put our feet as well as on that of our ancestors. I create sound structures that envelop everyone, also our plant and animal friends. With their participation, the right frequency spreads everywhere. I learn to perceive the structures I create better and better, and to check on them with the eyes of the dream. They look like strong and luminous spheres; they tune and orientate the vibration of everything to increase the harmony of the connection between us, the sky and mother Earth.

Together with our medicine men and women, and others who have powers within them, I strengthen and protect the paths along which the new souls reach us, and those of the dying leave: it's the same circle, a wheel that can continue to turn harmoniously if we give it our constant attention.

I have several children by strong women of my people. In one of them I see my same characteristics, so I ask the shaman to take him in right away. This is a gift to my people that makes me very proud.

One night I dream of the great eucalyptus tree, and I realize it's summoning me. I greet my family and my people according to our traditional rituals. I carry them all with me in my heart.

The journey to the tree is very long and challenging this time. Perhaps, it's me who is tired. I sit in contact with its trunk and little by little, I slow my heart down through breathing. The sound of my branch now is a long, deep, grateful salute to this land. I know I will return in the grandchildren of my grandchildren.

I'm ready to join my ancestors, and my transition is easy. I've traveled to the other world so many times before, and today I don't even have to worry about leaving the passage open for my return. The tree is alive and present also in this dimension, and under its crown once again I sit, greeted by sounds and whispers welcoming me.

A MISTAKE THAT CHANGED A DESTINY

Atlantis. Right after the Golden Age.

I programmed my rebirth myself. I knew the procedure very well: I had dedicated my entire previous existence to the study of the delicate mechanism to connect a soul to the right body to carry out its mission. Genetics had long made it possible to build a healthy body in a balanced way; our task was more delicate because the individual's happiness and usefulness to our great people depended on this connection. It was a job for a scientist-priest and, in my previous existence, I had manifested the appropriate qualities already as a child.

I learned to contact the gods who preside over the timelines directly, avoiding the many tedious steps of the intermediate Forces. For this, I had become famous. I recorded books and many holo-videos dedicated to my discovery. In spite of this, at the time of my death, few scientists could follow my method correctly. The procedure was not technical, but spiritual, and not everyone understood this.

Many scientists saw the gods only as great machines, sentient energy mechanisms, in relation to us only with precise, unchangeable functions.

On the contrary, I remembered the times when devotion was considered a fundamental element to connect humans and gods. It was a relationship of mutual communication and respect. In my opinion, it was precisely this that made it possible to create the best balance between soul, body and memory.

To make sure I wouldn't waste time on pointless research, I added devotion—a precious ingredient—in good quantities to the structure of my next life. I left for my next me everything that could be useful to awaken my memories fast. Serene, I left my old shell behind, waiting for the moment to be reborn. I planned for it not to be right away, so that a few generations would go by. I wanted to see where my discoveries would lead to, which new possibilities they'd open for my people. I wanted to be amazed!

The first surprise—one I really didn't expect—is my body! It was surely a joke by some co-scientist of mine, who altered the track of one little chromosome, and made me be born a woman. I don't mind it at all now, but it was a little tricky at first. I found everything my previous self had prepared for the full awakening of my memories—but nothing fully suitable to train a female human.

My brain functioned differently than he had expected. The codes I was reading to myself, the olfactory traces I was breathing, the sounds I had recorded in my previous life, were all specific to the male gender. They didn't activate the right chemistry in me, because the hormones in my bloodstream were different! How frustrating at first! I got very angry, I felt I was the victim of a hoax: I, the great expert, had failed to provide myself with the right tools to accomplish my mission!

Then I started to reflect. I realized that maybe it hadn't been a scientist's little joke, but a very rare natural possibility of variation. And if that was the case, then being a woman was actually part of the Program. I needed to explore what its potential was, not consider it a limitation. I gratefully thanked my former self, said goodbye to him, and put all his material back in the archives. Leaving the Corporation was easy. After all, I was an exception to them, which complicated things. My unpredicted anatomy made me free!

Unlike the previous me who practically lived in them, I don't like high-tech labs. The sense of the divine I feel in me is not technical at all, but a warm wave of joy and gratitude for life. The variation created me healthy and strong: what pleasure it is to feel my body, now that I know that my destiny is not already traced ahead of me. The predisposition towards science is strong within me, but just as powerful is my desire for a contact with the Soul of the world. This is the channel I want to explore, the deep frequency that orders life in this corner of space-time and makes it possible for us to breathe, dream and live.

To do this, I have to leave the capital, where I live in the area designated for scientists, and move to a region closer to the mountains. In that land there are still some cultivated areas on the surface, and large forest-gardens that provide valuable substances for healing and life.

With my Program credentials I'm admitted among their researchers. Here, too, they look for the connections between body and spirit, but not the human ones, those of the plant world. I quickly learn to get in touch with the frequencies of plants, to transfer their properties into preparations ready to receive them. There's no need to cut out any physical parts, we just use our mind as a bridge and then we transfer their healing properties.

It's an exciting work. In order to be recognized and accepted by the spirit of plants, we must also merge our lives with theirs. I spend many hours in the forest, taking care of the trees and the undergrowth, the springs and their waters. My hands are strong, I like to touch moss and dirt and often I have some left under my nails. This gives me great satisfaction: I carry a little piece of the Mother with me.

I am a mature researcher now and I feel a sense of urgency awakening in me, perhaps something left behind by my previous self. I have a special relationship with a pond of water at the foot of a spring. Its access code has long been discovered, and contact with its energy matrix is easy. I know how to use it to heal myself, to regenerate my body and mind. From here I get the idea for a new line of research: I want to find the frequency of the Force that unites all the waters, the vibration that can give access to all the memories that water holds. Its presence in our preparations would bring the remedies to a much greater level of power. I analyze the code of the Water Forces, break it down, reassemble it, add variables and write and rewrite the formula.

A team of researchers joins me, all trained for years in the contact-transmission of plant frequencies. We don't need to talk, our minds are connected just as our longings and determination are. It takes us a long time, but we succeed. We change the whole procedure for scanning and entering the frequencies in the distillates.

Our research is shared with many other laboratories, in other sectors, as Unified Frequency Waters are an invaluable basis for many different uses.

I'm satisfied. I've accomplished my Mission and I'm worthy of choosing a new incarnation within my people. I decide to let the Priestly Guild of New Directions choose for me. This time, I don't want to know beforehand where I will be reborn next. When I realize that the timeline of my current existence will not continue much longer, I forward my request to them, attaching my validated soul history, my self-assessment and my insights on what elements I could refine in a next life. This is required of, and granted to, everyone who has reached a sufficient level of self-mastery and awareness.

I choose to leave my body while it's still healthy and whole, in the warm embrace of the pond waters. I see it floating, my long auburn hair framing my face. The sun makes it as shiny as the colors of sunset. I feel so much love for this human form that gives glory to the divine, and walks with honor on this wonderful planet. I reach my destination quickly; I have traveled the path several times during my preparation.

AN ARCHITECT WHO SLID INTO THE SOUL OF A PRINCE

First Babylonian Empire. Times of King Hammurabi. Circa 1790 B.C.

When my consciousness enters the body I will use for my mission, I realize my task won't be easy. My people and the humans of this empire have signed a pact. Members of their royal family and their priests are aware of the stellar plan to reconnect Earth to the cosmic order, and have agreed to be in service to it.

The young man destined to be my human vessel has been carefully chosen from among the nobles. He's strong and healthy, and has already enjoyed many of the pleasures of human life. His education is also adequate to develop the basic skills I need. He's seventeen years old when I enter his soul structure: his spirit has accepted the task, though his human part is unaware of it.

The transfer occurs at the time of his biological birthday, so that his subtle bodies are aligned. It's a natural biorhythm that makes the process easier for both of us. His/my physical body suffers a fever for a few days, the time needed for me to connect my complex information structure to the life centers along his spine and the other energy systems in his body: in this way, my matrix will adapt to the one present in every human being of this planet. When he opens his eyes, fully healed, I'm ready, and my story begins.

My energetic imprint in the young nobleman is recognized and validated by the high priests. I am taken to the main temple where my connection and the memories needed for this mission can be completed. My preparation takes a few years. During that time I never leave the temple complex. I don't perceive time as humans do, so for me this is just a suspended period, completely dedicated to absorbing data and information.

I pass several levels of initiation, necessary to connect to the Forces that oversee this part of the space-time continuum, and I too become a priest. This is human language to indicate a high-level technician who knows how to operate the temples, the powerful devices connecting humans, lines of destiny and larger cosmic forces.

My job is to download complex codes and designs to use as the basis for the architectural structures of new temples and public buildings. Through their masses and symbols, energies and thoughts will be directed for millennia to come. I study ancient texts and musical patterns.

I observe the stars to receive insights and information. For many years I work on defining the geometries of a very large irrigation system, intended to harness and direct cosmic energies. The King is very cooperative and the system gets built, employing great resources.

The temples and structures I am having built will be a part of the beacon to direct the arrival of selected soul-people. Others like me are doing the same in other temples, in other times and other places. We have no connection to each other while we are on Earth: it is one of many safety procedures to make sure the plan proceeds without interference or danger.

I never let anyone touch me, and I have no interest in sex that absorbs so much energy and attention from humans. Yet, as time goes by, I come to love this place and I enjoy being in this body. I spend long hours in the gardens, and enjoy every pleasure my senses can give me: the exquisite scents of flowers, the surprising taste of fresh water, the infinite melody of nature, the incredible diversity of all the birds and insects, the ever-changing colors of the sky...

My expanded senses allow me to pick up signals and stimuli that activate new capacities in my brain.

I can see multiple planes of reality, different probabilities of events. Mostly, I use my abilities to provide data to my people. A couple of times, I use my foresight to help the King refine his war strategies so that my works are not endangered. I cannot take sides in human affairs, I intervene only as a protector of our millennial plan to sow and nurture civilizations.

I can extend my perceptions far beyond the walls of the temple complex, and feel the waves of human emotion coming from the city. I never have any desire to throw myself into it. So much confusion, so little awareness. Humans are still like frantic ants without the ability to choose for themselves.

Approximately twenty years go by, and the time comes to terminate my mission. The intense use of the brain has worn down the body I'm using. I leave during a solar eclipse. When I re-enter the network of my people, I don't feel any time has passed. My host lives a few more years, then he dies with no memories and no pain. His willingness to participate in the Plan grants him a new life with greater awareness.

A PAINTER AND HER PRECIOUS PIGMENTS

Italy. Areas of Umbria and Tuscany. Sixteenth century.

I love the green, rolling hills of my land. The paintings in which I depict them are my favorite. I am the only daughter of a well-known painter, and I literally grow up in his atelier. My mother tries to say that, since I am a girl, it would be better for me to stay home and help her. Luckily, my father thinks otherwise. He recognizes my talent already when I'm a child, and decides I have the right to follow in his footsteps. To me, my father is the most wonderful man in the world.

I'm curious and have an exceptional visual memory. I don't talk much, but I love to sing while drawing. I feel that the energy of my breath, modulated through a song, helps my hand glide lightly and confidently across the paper. My father trains me together with his other apprentices, demanding the same attention and devotion from me.

I'm eager to learn. It takes a lot of work just to keep the store tidy, make lists of supplies, mix the spices for the sweet wine he offers his customers... Later, I learn how to prepare the canvases, and I start painting parts of my father's works, filling in with color the outlines of clothes and landscapes, skies and mountains...

I enjoy observing the wide range of characters coming to commission work. I can guess what they'll ask for from the expression on their faces and the movements of their bodies: the man in love who wants a portrait of his lover; the politician wanting to be depicted to show off his power; the noblewoman who wants her little dog to keep her company forever, at least on canvas... People amuse and interest me. I keep a notebook with sketches of all our customers. I start drawing them as a girl, and continue throughout my time in my father's studio. It's my tribute to the women and men of my town.

I work hard as an apprentice for several years, then finally my father decides to teach me the secrets of making the colors that helped make him famous. His paintings are brighter than those of his competitors, the light seems to shine through and out of the canvas. It's a special mixture of ground stones and tree resins, which must be boiled and filtered, and then added to rare and precious pigments in the right amount. If I put too much of the mixture, the paint on the canvas will crack and peel; if there's too little there's no shine.

I experiment eagerly, and master the technique very quickly. I want to apply a touch of these bright pigments also to faces, to emphasize certain expressions. The first portraits I make are those of my father and the other apprentices. The outcome leaves them very surprised... and rather disconcerted. Their faces seem to move as the light changes, and they don't have the look of austere solemnity we're accustomed to. My father decides to put some of them on display anyway, to see if they catch the eye of his customers. The portraits sit there, gathering dust for three years, and I simply continue to complete parts of my father's works.

One day, a group of very elegant men arrive from Florence, looking for a stone mason for a new building. They walk into the store, so confidently that they seem a bit arrogant. They're intrigued by the portraits. When my father says I was the one who painted them, one of the men immediately says he wants one made, too. He looks at me with such intensity he makes me blush. He wants me to follow him to Florence, and work there. I'm a little afraid to leave, but he offers such a large sum of money that my father cannot refuse.

I'm assigned a spacious and luminous room in a secondary wing of a large and ornate building.

I have a small garden, quiet despite the chaos of the city, where I spend many happy hours reading and testing the brightness of my colors. I have a personal attendant and I am also given clothes, much more elegant than the simple tunics I'm used to wearing. There is a dress in dark green velvet that I like very much. I know how difficult it is to get that special shade, the fabric is so precious I feel like a noblewoman just touching it. It's the one I wear in the portrait I'll paint of myself several years later.

Capturing the spirit of my patron on the canvas is more complex and difficult than I expected. He has an impetuous temperament, he changes moods often and this alters his features and even the color of his eyes. I struggle to paint a portrait truly resembling him; he's not happy with the result, and my plan to return home as soon as possible goes up in smoke.

I change strategy, I relax and don't worry about capturing anything anymore. I simply breathe, watch him and sing while I paint. His attitude changes, too: in the intimate space full of light and smells of my studio, I discover love and passion. I feel the need to be as close to him as possible, mixing the moments of day and night as if they were the colors of my palette.

Little by little, we make our relationship public, and I discover a whole new world. I accompany him to meetings and dinners and my mind opens up more and more, absorbing the new ideas that everyone in town is discussing. Everything seems to be ready to be born anew, reinvented, reconsidered. New discoveries, new technologies, a new era: I live in the city that is at the center of it all!

The relationship with my patron lasts several years. Then, little by little, he gently disappears from my bed and from my life. By now Florence has become my home, and I'm happy to enjoy it alone. I have plenty of work, and I feel the master of my own life. I still don't like talking much, but I participate passionately in debates about art.

I think we artists need to be free, to be able to search a person's soul without the constraint of religion. This is a debate that makes tempers flare, and it can be dangerous at times. Not everyone in town shares such liberal views.

I dedicate myself completely to my art for a long time. Love comes gently back into my life with a young woman, a painter like me. She reminds me of what I was like when I started to really live. I gladly teach her all my secrets, and we share ideas and dreams.

She's very talented, and it's a joy for me to see her grow artistically. We often collaborate on the same work, painting many noble families and laughing as we imagine the hidden life of each of their members.

Our joy is the special ingredient that makes our works come alive. She's by my side for the rest of my life, a sweet, reliable and optimistic companion.

I die shortly after turning forty, during a frigid winter, having spent too much time painting in the cold. My beloved is by my side. The last joy of my life is seeing the glow of the first rays of the morning sun on her honey-colored hair.

A SHEIKH WITH A SECRET TO PROTECT

Arab countries. Oasis. About 1100.

My whole life revolves around a secret. And the irony is, this secret is not mine.

My father died prematurely when I was little more than a boy. Since then, I have been in control of everything in this part of the desert. My father's assassination—I'm sure that's what it was, even though the attack was well disguised and I could never prove it—could have caused a big division, but I quickly took power by securing the loyalty of the most powerful clan leaders; I even managed to expand our area of influence.

This is a rich region, full of trades, people, cultures, music and beauty. I feel I'm the son of this land, free and proud like all its people. I have great energy and a strong and optimistic character. My life is always in motion. I prefer to live in my tent, rather than at the palace. I make decisions quickly, and without giving them a second thought. I have only one word, and everyone knows better than to go against it.

I love everything under this clear sky, which suddenly disappears to give way to untamable sand storms, hiding everything in an unstoppable whirlwind.

This is also the description of the landscape of my heart. I keep this secret, but my feelings on this matter are always in turmoil. I've had to change my life, shift its center from myself and my clan to something else that I have to consider more important and more valuable. Without clearly knowing why.

I wasn't given much choice. They arrived on horseback, like so many others, but as soon as they entered my tent I realized these men were different. I had heard stories about them, but I thought they were one of the many legends the wind carries, tales made more vivid at each bivouac.

They had no fear of me, and that was strange enough. There was no one, for many days' journey from my oasis, who did not know that a word of mine could mean life or death. I never had anyone killed, but preventing caravans from passing through my lands forced merchants to follow a much longer and dangerous way. My grandfather secured our clan's control over that route, and our power has never been challenged since. These knights looked me in the eye as an equal; actually, perhaps there was even a slight sense of superiority in their gaze. I pretended not to notice it, I welcomed them and listened. I’ve heard many stories, and I also enjoy telling them, but what they told me was really fascinating.

They talked of a war of conquest for treasures of such inestimable value to transform the whole world. They told me of great castles in Europe, routes to connect them, knowledge more valuable than any jewel.

I followed everything with great attention, but more than what I heard with my ears I was struck by what I perceived in my mind: a sort of irresistible calling making me accept everything as true, a force that won't let me say no when they told me I must help. They wanted me to be the guardian of something of enormous value, something I must commit to protecting at the cost of my life. Something that, much later, they'll come to take back.

I didn't expect it to be a child. His skin is much lighter than ours, almost like the skin of slaves from the countries of wind and rain. His eyes are dark and intense like those of the Prophet. He's probably four years old, but what I read in his look is much more ancient. A mixture of wisdom and images of the horrors he escaped from. I must never tell anyone who brought him to me; I must protect and instruct him as if he were the son of a king; and train him as a fighter. I cannot ask who he is, nor why he is here. Nor for how long he will stay.

The knights depart, and I feel furious for agreeing to this. Surely this is a dangerous matter, and the little boy's presence will change many things. I need to set up a fake raid to make it look like he's part of a battle spoils, and then choose him for my quarters.

My task is to educate him and this, too, requires a plan. I choose a first wife, and we have a son. Now it's totally normal for me to select a group of trainers and nannies. The two children live together in a wing of the palace, surrounded by guards. They are all sworn to secrecy.

My young guest doesn't speak much; he's obedient and well disposed. I give him a name in my language. I hire instructors for math, poetry, music, astrology, combat, caravan and exploration techniques.

A few years go by, and I start to think that maybe this story isn't real. I'm having trouble at a border, so I take a few guards off the boys' watch. I need more soldiers at the frontier, and I've probably exaggerated with the protection for my guest. Some days later, a few men on horseback arrive at the oasis. I don't need them to be announced to know who they are. They leave a book for my young guest, and a warning, made up only of glances, for me.

Arrivals and deliveries of books and items for the young man repeat over the next twelve years, and the knights never catch me unprepared again.

The boys grow up, my son is fond of our guest, and I love them both. I feel pride and pleasure in watching them grow into young, strong and principled men. I personally teach them strategy, and how to read into the souls of men. We pray together, and together we discuss the mysteries of the universe.

My life becomes more settled, I no longer travel with the caravans for long periods. I want to be close to that young man: everything I teach him is a way to leave something of me in him, to participate in the project of which he's a part. His presence has a note of great wisdom and strength. I see the positive influence he has on my children, the first one and the others who arrived over the years, and I am grateful for that. I am truly forging kings.

The day he leaves the oasis is one of the saddest of my life. No words are needed, I can tell by his embrace that the time has come. He has an appointment. I have him escorted to the desert gate; once there, he sends my men back. For months I look at the stars wondering if the pattern they draw is showing the fulfillment of his destiny.

I don't think I'll ever see the treasures the knights told me about, but the whisper of the stars are intimations of a greater plan.

I pour all my love on my first son, who grows up to be nobler and more courageous than I ever was. This gives me great joy. I leave him the kingdom as soon as I feel he's ready to rule it. I retreat to a private house on the edge of the oasis.

I spend my time immersed in my studies. Surrounded by silence, I listen to the voice of the wind. Finding out what the Great Plan is becomes my most important goal.

I die at sunset, on a day in which the wind is so strong that it takes my breath away. I am old. I ask Allah to allow me not to forget what I've understood.

A SEER LOVED BY A GOD

Ancient times. Eriu (modern Ireland). Epoch of the Druids.

I was born during a winter storm. I have a mark on my shoulder that resembles the antlers of a deer. Indeed, a herd of deer had gathered around the hut where my mother brought me into this world. It was a simple dwelling partly made of wood, partly a moss-covered cave. The priests were praying around my mother, knowing she would die to get me there, to open the passage to my essence. She had seen it herself, in one of her visions. She could choose to accept the sacrifice or refuse it and continue living, but she had no hesitation. The druids made sure my aura was strong and my body healthy to receive her great inheritance at birth, while the ritual to connect her spirit to the Sacred Oak began.

My training starts as a child. I play with bones and stones for divination; my playmates are the spirits of the forest that I must learn to summon to gain their respect. I keep the fire going and fetch water from the river. Little by little I am taught how to talk to the elements of nature.

I live in a protected area, a little far from the village. It's a space dedicated to the sacred people. There, we tend a garden of magical plants, and there are underground caves where we guard the holy fire and perform the rituals that keep us connected to Mother Earth and her soul. In return, she helps us live in a dimension other than the physical one, a space where we can see her subtle forces. We learn to talk to them, respecting and loving them. They protect us and give us health, food and happy dreams. They open the doors to powerful visions.

I'm tall, my hair is long and darker than that of most of my people. My eyes have the color of the summer moss. When my body changes, and I become capable of giving life, a crescent moon is tattooed on my forehead, as a symbol of my dedication to the Powers. At this moment, my life changes, and I become who I was born to be for my people, for our safety, for our world.

I prepare for months for my first Sacred Union. I spend a lot of time reciting incantations, shifting my mind onto a different plane of reality; I contemplate the moon; I bathe in the ritual pond and take long walks in the forest. I drink the infusion of the sacred herbs that purify my body and open my spirit. When the time for the celebration comes, I'm ready.

The drums have been beating for a few nights when I receive the dream. I open my eyes and there is no difference from what I was dreaming.

The first priestess stands next to me in my hut. She helps me wash and put on the ritual headpiece of fur and beads made of painted bones and walnut shells. I lace up my long shoelaces and wrap myself in a fur cloak.

When I reach the central fire, where everyone is dancing, I see a man coming towards me. He wears a magnificent headdress made from the antlers of a mighty deer. As he comes closer, he gets bigger and more luminous: he is the God of the Forest. When he touches me, the light from the fire becomes very bright and the drums carry us far away. I can still hear them, but only as a background noise in the distance.

Our physical union gives me such ecstasy that I feel my spirit reconnect to the universe from whence I came. The celebration lasts a few nights, and many times I unite with the God. It's all like one long dream. The gift of my pure life force nourishes him, and he will grant fertility to humans and nature. The gift for me, as my mother foretold, is that of vision.

I never touch a man for the rest of my life. My energy belongs to the God, and he summons me deep into the forest when he wants me to unite with him. He never manifests again in human form.

I perceive him coming, and then it's just an embrace of light and energy. I feel myself being transported into the cosmos again, and there I can travel forward with the sun and moon. I see the dangers—both physical and in the realm of spirits—awaiting my people, the events that are going to happen. As time goes by, I learn to move along the lines that carry all destinies, and I see their connecting threads. I can foresee deaths and births, so that my people can prepare for them.

The forest is a happy place, full of voices and sentient beings. The trees have a powerful presence and hold the memories of our ancestors. They often come with me in my explorations along the destiny lines. I learn to ask them for help in opening new passages and dimensions. My heart fills with compassion and love as I feel the essence of other people's lives flowing through me. I am grateful for my life, my gift, my people. I am appreciated and loved.

I die in the winter. I'm ready, and a younger woman has prepared to take my place. Once again the deer gather around my hut. I feel my spirit pass through one of them, for one last quick jump before going through the Door.

A HORSE BREEDER AND THE KING'S SOUP

Spain. Kingdom of Philip V. Beginning of the eighteenth century.

The smell of the stables and the scent of the vegetable soup always simmering on the big stone fireplace accompany me all my life; they remind me of who I am, and what is truly important.

I'd never thought that one day I'd share a dish of that very soup with the King himself—sometimes life offers unexpected gifts. There was just me there that day, listening to a man with a soul tormented by intrigue and betrayal, carrying a burden greater than he felt he could bear. It was just a quick moment, but enough to give me an insight on the true values of life: its echo has stayed with me ever since. And I've told the story so many times, to my family, to the villagers, to my grandchildren, that I always have the impression all this happened just yesterday. And yet, so many years have gone by...

I was born in the forest, in my family's large stone farmhouse. We've been breeding horses for the royal family for generations. The work is hard and times are difficult due to the constant wars; often payments are late, and we don't have much to eat; other times, if the sovereigns are particularly happy with the horses we send, they send gifts and we can celebrate with the whole village. We are a small, close-knit community, we all know and help each other like one big family.

My mother dies when I'm only four years old. Two women in the village take care of me and my three siblings. They seem to compete for who's more loving with us. When I grow older, I understand it's my father's heart they want to win, but he never makes a choice, and so we are often all together around the same table.

My father is a strong, outspoken, sociable man with a big heart. He loves his horses as much as he loves us. He teaches us that in order to tame them we must respect them, know them, feel what they feel, and perceive what they think.

Since I was a child, I've spent many nights in the barn, lying on the straw next to the foals, enduring the cold of winter and the torment of the flies in summer. My father is adamant about this: he says we must be completely in tune with them, till we dream the same dreams. My siblings make jokes about this, but I think it's possible.

As I grow up and learn to take care of the horses better and better, I begin to perceive flashes of different thoughts in my mind: it's a sensation that starts on my skin and then becomes an idea, a more complete perception. I begin to give the horses orders with my mind, inviting them to come towards me, to follow me, to move as I indicate. I use my voice very little, only to mark the points of contact we reach. I get great results, I'm full of enthusiasm and I don't mind the long, tiring hours of work.

I ride very well, but what I love most is being with the horses in the stables and in the corral, me on my two legs and them on their four: man and animals who respect and learn from each other. Above all, I love being of help at birthing time, the arrival of a foal is always a gift from God. Over time, I learn to assist pregnant mares, and help them give birth by myself.

My father is very proud of me, and I'm happy to take over his duties more and more. My older brothers, however, decide to leave and work for the royal shipyards that are always looking for men. My younger brother, less strong and independent, stays with me. I take care of him, as if he were my son, all his life.

I get married very young to a girl I've known since I was a boy. She brings sunshine into my life even on the grayest of days.

She's a hard worker, like me, and loves to sing. We have seven children, and the birth of the last one—finally a girl!—steals her away from me.

I'm furious with God. Darkness takes over my heart. I spend a few weeks alone with the horses; I don't go back home and I don't talk to anyone. I hardly eat and I look like a ghost. Then, light slowly begins to return to my soul; one day, I wake up and have the impression of seeing my wife in front of the fireplace, standing as she did every morning, with her long brown hair not yet gathered. She smiles sweetly at me and fades away. I feel she wants me to go on with my life.

I pour my love on my children raising them as I was raised; I'm very proud that all of them, also my daughter, have the skills, sensitivity and strength to continue my work.

I don't like to sleep in an empty bed, but for a long time I choose to have only occasional companions. Only ten years after the death of my wife do I decide to remarry; I've developed a deep affection for a younger woman who takes care of me with devotion. She's a good mother to my children, and we have two more. She gives me serenity and new energy: I feel young again.

I live a long, serene life, full of affection, work, commitment, emotions, flavors, colors and scents. I feel at peace with myself and with God.

I die in my late sixties from an infection, probably caused by a rusty nail. During the fevers of my last days, I think often again of the King, in his wonderful palace... my heart tells me that between the two of us, I was the luckier, the one given a happy life and true freedom.

A LETTER THAT WAS NEVER SENT

Ancient China. Imperial city.

I am a royal princess. I've been told so many times that every part of my mind, my body, and my soul have learned what it means, what everyone expects from me: perfection, obedience and silence. Mine is a powerful family, we rule and conquer, our land is so vast that it goes from the sea to the mountains, our soldiers are so many that a moon cycle would not suffice to count them all. But our enemies are also many, the emperor is unpredictable, his men treacherous and corrupt. I'm a precious instrument in the hands of my family.

I'm exceptionally beautiful, the result of well-planned marriages of our men to the most lovely women of the country over many generations. Nothing in my life is left to chance, even before it began. Yet, something peculiar happened anyway, something they didn't expect. I wasn't born alone, a twin brother came into the world right after me. I feel his presence near me; I've had recurring dreams of him for many years, I know he's alive somewhere.

Why is he kept away? Why isn't he here with me, with his family? I soon learn that asking questions leads to nothing but lies and punishment.

But that only makes my determination to find him stronger. I feel I must find him to make sense of my life, only his existence can free mine.

I follow the rules, I play my role, I learn to be perfect in every moment. I find peace and harmony in the beauty of my gardens, a magnificent work of art of colors and scents. I love to walk among the flowers and medicinal plants to gather my thoughts. I breathe deeply and then sit down: when I reach a point of absolute calm inside me, I feel transported to another place. The scents bring me sensations and images of a different setting, as if I were looking through different eyes. I sense weapons and masters, discipline, strong winds and a monastery high up on a mountain. I know that I'm seeing what my twin sees.

It takes years, but I finally gather enough information to understand what happened: my brother is hidden for political reasons, no one must know my dynasty has a second male heir. He's a secret weapon, to be used in case the firstborn is killed in an attempt to take power away from our family.

I begin to map out a plan to find him. I feel it's my task and my duty to rescue him from the isolation he's in. I don't want to believe it's impossible!

I'm a young woman now, and I'm married to a powerful and very wealthy man. He's much older and so enamored of me that he yields to my desires much more than anyone in my family ever did. I have a new extension built to his mansion and wonderful new gardens where I can reflect and make plans in absolute privacy.

There's such a constant flow of money that I can secretly use some of it to pay for a new network of informants. They'll discover where my brother is. I know it's a very risky game, but I'm not afraid. In great secrecy I also begin to organize a caravan for the trip. I'll find a way to escape: one thing at a time, I'll overcome all obstacles. My connection with my twin in dreams, fueled by my strong hopes and all the new information, becomes more vivid. Sometimes I can even hear his voice, perceive his presence near me. I convince myself that he feels mine too: with him I have the deepest dialogues. He's my best friend, I feel complete only in our connection.

One night I have a terrible nightmare. I feel my heart split into two, and in the morning I can't feel my contact with him. I look for him among my flowers; I send him my thoughts, my prayers, my tears: nothing, I perceive no reply. I understand he has been killed.

Someone else must have been investigating my secret, and they were quicker than I.

I feel a part of me dies with my brother. There's a hole in my heart and life is slipping out through it, little by little. I become a shadow of what I was. There's a bleak silence in my mind, over which I cannot cultivate any happy thoughts. I cannot sleep, I have no desire to eat, I wander helplessly in my gardens. Only their beauty can alleviate my pain, but little by little even their colors become less luminous, their scents fade...

My husband is desperate, he can't understand what's happening. He calls the best doctors in all of our great empire. His deep love and care touch my heart, but it's too late, I have no more energy or will to live.

I die on a beautiful spring morning, holding the letter I wrote for my brother announcing my arrival to save him.

A MAN WHO LOOKED THE SUN IN THE EYE

Northern Africa. Ancient times.

We are the children of the Sun. We learn to look into its eyes from childhood. The priests give us sacred ointments to smear around our eyes, so that the Sun doesn't blind us, giving us the gift of seeing the light in all things.

We are a small people, living in an area of lush vegetation, just beyond the caves in the rocks. Our elders say it was our special sight that made our ancestors find it, no one else can see this place. We have water and raise sheep, and we grow fruit trees and grains. Our women tend the plants with respect and love, as if they were children.

We are a very old tribe, and just as ancient are our customs. We have great respect for our women that bring the gift of life; for the elders; for all the elements of nature. Already as children, we men learn to fight to defend our land; in order to keep it a secret, we trade in a different place, where caravans come, keeping far away from our settlement. We have something everyone wants, a special spice that gives men the power of a horse, the fire of a big cat, and the keen senses of an eagle. Our women make it, taking it from the seeds and bark of a tree.

It's our treasure, a sacred plant the Sun has given us to make us prosper. We know how to use it well; we start taking a little bit of it as children to develop our sight.

We're trained to always be in control of ourselves: those who are too proud to have the patience to learn become blind and must leave. This is the price you pay if you are not respectful of the force, like many men of the other tribes: they cannot control the spirit of the medicine, and always crave more. We see them coming to our tent like thirsty wanderers to a pond in the desert. Their spirit is weak, there's no light in their soul. We don't let them stay near us long.

I'm one of the best at transactions: I can close a deal with just one glance of my deep, dark eyes, and instinctively discern the better goods. I'm particularly capable of selecting swords and knives. It feels as if metals speak to me: I know which ones have light in them and can become the seat of a special power. Metals are a gift from the Sun: its heat releases their force from deep within Mother Earth. They must be treated with respect.

Our artisans take any metal object we bring to them, and transform it with their art, etching ancient sacred symbols onto their surfaces.

Some of these objects become simply beautiful, others turn magical, like the knives we keep for ourselves. We use them in our ceremonies: they connect us to the Sun, they make its power flow through our bodies.

It's mostly men who own a magical knife, but also some of our women: the grandmothers preserving the memories of our tribe, the mothers of the most honorable men, sometimes even the young priestesses of the House of the Sun. It's a large cave, where a fire is always lit, right under an opening that lets in the rays of the sun.

In the cavern, my people sing and play to the rhythm of ancient drums, dancing ecstatically to give praise to the Sun. In those moments, I feel its light enter my body so deeply that I lose all sense of who I am. I become a ray of sunlight; I feel the music moving me; I trace signs turning around in circles while the knife, which I hold up high in my hand, becomes the magic wand connecting me with my Father.

It's in the cave that I choose the woman who will be my partner. I see the light shining through her knife so clearly that I know she's the one I need to give birth to my children, our gifts to all our people.

She is a young Priestess, and I know that our times together will be governed by the movements of the Sun and Moon, but I accept this with a light heart. I know I can find warm companionship in other arms, but I don't perceive her radiance in anybody else. We have two sons and a daughter.

The boys are raised by the tribe, as per tradition, while my daughter joins her mother in the House of the Sun, as she has the birthmark of the priestesses. I'm grateful to the Sun that gave me the opportunity to serve my people with this union.

I live a long and happy life. I learn to look into the heart of the Sun and perceive the Door. When the time comes to leave my tired and worn out body, I am ready. I know this life is a step, this land is a station: my soul is preparing for another mission. I'm lying on my mat, with my magic knife beside me. Its power aids me in the transition, as I hear the drums of the House of the Sun greeting the birth of another day.

A GIRL PLAYING THE FLUTE ON THE ANDES

High Andes. Sixteenth century.

My mother told me she was chanting while giving birth to me. I'm the youngest of many children, and it was easy for her to bring me into the world. She said she felt no pain, but a sense of joy so deep that it made her sing. She knew I came carrying a gift for our people. What that was, it was up to me to find out.

We are a small and close-knit people. Everyone is always busy, men and women. We treat each other with great respect and have many occasions to celebrate. We love to wear bright, many-hued clothes, as colors represent the nuances and emotions of life, to be all shared through music and celebrations.

I am petite, but strong and resilient. My grandfather teaches me to control my breathing from an early age. He says that at these altitudes, here where the sky caresses the mountains, breath is the secret of life and happiness. It's the connection to our past and our future. It brings inside of us the stories the winds tell, to remind us of who we are, of our rightful place on this Earth. And our land is sacred, because the winged gods lived here once. We can no longer see them, but their images are engraved high on some of the mountain walls, near large stone platforms. We know they used them to land here. We know they will return to reunite with our Great Mother Earth.

Like many in my family I learn to play the flute. Something special happens when I breathe into it for the first time. I feel the air around me responding to my sound. It seems that the wind spirits recognize my melody, as if it were a language. My grandfather smiles and encourages me to experiment. I walk alone for long distances, on high altitude trails, looking for a method to summon the forces of the air.

At first it's a bit of a game, but as time goes on I take it much more seriously. I play and then stop and listen: I hear the voices of the spirits up there in the sky more and more clearly. I search for the right sounds to communicate with all these forces, and also to be heard by the mountain. She's our ancient mother, our sacred home. When she finally chooses to answer me, I know my training is over, I'm ready for my task. Now I must use my gift for others.

Terrifying stories start reaching our village from far away on the plains, and even from greater distances, all the way from the people of the sea.

They tell of monsters and angry gods coming to the shores of our world. They bring death and chaos. Their powerful, evil magic enters even the dreams of our shaman, and turn them into nightmares. He warns us that we must keep them away. The wise men of our tribe sometimes see their horrible faces in the pond with the sacred waters. They look like human beings, but we are sure they're not.

I understand what I am to do. Every day I walk high up the mountain to a rock cliff where a small cave protects me from the fierce winds. From there I can see my village, my people, our animals, the small plots of cultivated land all around. My heart fills with love and the desire to protect everything. I play my flute weaving a special bubble of protection around everyone. I know it will take me a long time to complete my work and make it truly resilient, but I feel ready for it.

I chew the leaves of our allied plant and focus all my strength on summoning the spirits to help me; I prepare offerings to the gods. I often offer them a few drops of my blood with the promise of giving them all my life force. I won't marry, nor will I have children. I will belong only to the spirits, in life and after death.

The shaman helps me and after a few moons, he tells me the gods have accepted my offer. I feel my power increase incredibly. I perceive and see the bubble I create: it will keep all invaders away. At night, I sleep deeply and my dreams are peaceful.

I share my optimism with everyone, and I often manage to bring a smile back to my people's faces. The monsters won't come all the way up here; the mountain will protect us. I receive so much love and gratitude from everyone that I never feel lonely, I don't regret making my choice.

A full cycle of the sun hasn't passed yet when a strong gust of wind snatches the flute from my hands. I run to pick it up, but I slip and begin to fall down the mountain. As I fly down, once again the beauty of my land touches my heart.

My spirit leaves my body before I crash on the rocks, and I feel no pain. On the other side there's light and Presence, and from there I can see very clearly the protection I've built. I am grateful for my life and happy to leave this gift to my people.

AN HERBALIST WHO KNEW NO BOUNDARIES

Ancient China. Imperial city.

Nothing in my life is conventional. This is what the stars intended for me, and I followed their direction, with a creative touch of personal interpretation. I'm not sure where I was born; some say in the secret of the royal gardens, others say it was right here, behind the busy market district. Either way, the color of my skin, lighter than everybody else's, and my above average height, indicate there's an exotic streak in me.

What I remember most about my early years is the strong scent of spices from the store where I grew up. The elderly herbalist and his wife adopted me and taught me their trade. I learned to distinguish the properties of plants by their shape and smell already as a child. The herbalist, whom I love like a father, is one of those who believe I have noble origins. He thinks I'm a gift from the gods, since he has no heir to pass his store on to. He wants me to have an education worthy of a mandarin... or almost, at least. I like to study, I learn fast, and he's very proud of me.

As I grind and weigh herbs for the concoctions we sell, a myriad of questions run through my mind. What gives a root its specific shape?

How is it possible that the same herb can have such extreme opposite effects as to either heal or kill a human body? I know there must be a general pattern connecting everything, creating a constant dance of relationships. I begin to get a taste of it by studying mathematics, and then astronomy, astrology, and the secrets of the energy lines of the human body. There I finally find the marriage between the physical and the invisible. I'm so excited that sleep almost disappears from my life!

I want to understand the relationship between all the possible fates of people and the healing plants. My beloved father laughs saying I'm crazy: it must be that strange bloodline of mine giving me such absurd ideas... I just know there's a connection, that planets have an intelligence that comes from an even greater design, and in the attraction and clash of their qualities we can find the space granted to us to lead our lives—to heal or perish.

I observe and catalog, take measurements and then use my intuition to perceive what I've theorized. I try many herbs at different times, in conjunction with astronomical phenomena, and search for their meaning deep within the symbols of the stars and the planets. I write and write and talk about my theories with all our clients.

At first, my father is afraid I'll scare them away, but then some start asking for consultations with me. I'm very excited to be able to test my theories on others, and not just myself.

I know I'm doing something unique, so I want to set myself apart from all the other healers: I have a special tunic made, in beautiful silk and with fine embroidery of the night sky. On the edges of the sleeves are the main medicinal plants of our tradition. It's a work of art and it boosts my self-confidence, making me feel like a prince. Underneath, I wear tunics of different colors, to give my magnetic field the right direction for each specific task. This way I can counterbalance any adverse astrological position. My clients are impressed by my regal and authoritative appearance and listen to me with reverence. Fortunately, my advice also work well, and I truly become an expert—I don't just look like one!

As time goes by, I hear more and more of the plant spirits speaking to me, showing me how they may intertwine with a particular life path. There's always a choice, nothing is fixed. I often see several possible outcomes, and feel the burden of choosing which ones to reveal, which energies to connect. This is my great responsibility.

I create new combinations all the time to expand my senses. I learn to let my body rest, and move into the beautiful matrix of light, connecting the living minds of planets and plants. I love pottery, and all of the pots for my herbs are works of art. I commission them myself, and discuss the designs with the artisans. Each one has to give a specific imprint on the herbs. They are vessels for a precious essence, and only beauty can have that honor.

I have children and three beautiful companions, who give me much joy and pleasure. I leave it to them to run the store I inherited, and to decide what to do with the wealth that is now flowing my way.

I die old, during one of my explorations with the help of a powerful plant. I knew it was likely to happen, the stars had told me so. I’ve written my will, and I leave everything in order. I'm very excited to discover how far I can travel now that I don't need to go back inside my body.

A YOUNG DAUGHTER OF RA
Ancient Egypt. 1400 BC.

I was born into a noble family, and I am destined for the temple. My parents know that this will be my destiny since before my birth: as soon as I am weaned from the nurse, they'll have to entrust me to a priestess and never see me again.

I grow up immersed in a sacred environment; my days flow at the pace of rituals and prayers, music and dance. The rhythms of life follow those of the moon and the sun, and through them my body and soul tune to the cycles of the cosmos..

The vegetation in this part of Egypt is lush, and all around the temple there are magnificent gardens, full of water, flowers and plants of all kinds. I love to spend as much time as possible there, walking around, breathing in the fragrant scent of the flowers and listening to the songs of the many birds that live there. I make friends with a parrot that spends a lot of time perched on my shoulder.

I'm always in a good mood, happy with my life. I really enjoy communicating with everyone and my relationships with the other girls and teachers are harmonious, which helps me focus fully on my studies. They teach us many subjects: the movement of the stars, the different reactions of metals, how to catalog and use herbs and powders. I have a quick mind and I like to study, so I learn everything fast. I know that I must follow the program that has been established for me, with dedication and constancy.

I am petite, my skin has a light amber color, and my hair is black and shiny. My body is strong and agile: my physical fitness is as important as that of my mind and spirit. I follow a vegetarian diet based on honey, dates, small round loaves of bread with dried fruit and pure gold in small amounts. My rest and wake times are regulated, and I exercise also in my sleep. I learn to move my double in the dream world, and I receive instructions from there, too.

I learn many kinds of languages, including secret ones—and the power of silence. I'm accustomed from an early age to keeping everything I do and learn a complete secret. I know I must be aware of every sound I make. Words have the power of creation, and now that mine are strong I must be able to control their effect.

When the moon transforms me into a woman and my body is ready to give life, my learning is complete.

Now I can move on to the operational phase, for which I prepared all these years. I leave the almost entirely feminine world where I lived until now, to begin operating with priests and magicians. Even though my life changes, everything feels natural; I'm guided by a deep and wise presence within me.

I have a new initiation, which consecrates me to Ra. I feel the energy of the Cosmic Sun transforming my cells, bringing even more light into my heart. I understand It's a Force extending far beyond my time, beyond my world. My people now have the role of keeping It connected to the Earth and to all humanity, but the Design is much greater. It's a path of return, of memories, energies and possibilities the frequency of this Force sustains until every particle of consciousness is fully recomposed. I'm aware of the great honor and responsibility I now have before our people and the lesser gods. They are all levels of consciousness that must be kept connected and ordered, so that everything on Earth can live and grow in harmony.

I have important tasks to perform, and I do so with joy and a spirit of dedication. My well-balanced energetic alchemy is appreciated in rituals, and I participate in increasingly complex magical operations. After some time, the head priest chooses me as his assistant.

I follow him in amazement along a yellowish-red stone corridor that leads to an underground citadel. He wears a tunic of white linen finer than mine, with shiny gold appliqués. His head is shaved. He's only a few years older than me, but his being exudes such confidence and authority that I would follow him anywhere. The slabs of stones are cool beneath my feet; the air is fragrant and rich with sounds coming from spaces I cannot see.

There are more-than-human-sized images of deities painted on the walls, and statues all along the corridor. We walk on rounded rocks to cross a large tank full of snakes; I see many servants with their tongues cut out so that they cannot reveal the existence of this place to anyone. They bow slightly as we pass.

We arrive in front of a large stone door, which slides open thanks to a secret mechanism. We enter a big alchemy laboratory. We're underground, yet the space is bright and well ventilated. The walls are covered in gold, and the laboratory is comfortable and well organized. It contains objects of a very advanced technology of our distant past; there are metals I don't recognize, artifacts that don't belong to our time. They come from an era of splendor that ended in catastrophe; we hold the memory of it.

Thanks to our work, the souls of that epoch won't be lost in the ocean of time, but will come back to meet one another again, in different moments, till a final appointment. At that time, every being will comprehend fully the meaning of their existence within the divine plan.

There are large metal and stone sarcophagi in which I spend a lot of time, leaving my physical body safe while I perfect my astral travel techniques. My journeys are very powerful. I learn to recognize and cross dimensional passages opened by burnished metal mirrors and sound frequencies reflected by the metal. I'm given precise destinations in time and in ancient astral libraries left behind by human and star peoples.

When I return, I bring useful elements to share with the priests; at times, they communicate them also to the King and the royal architects. They are information and sounds to be transformed into numbers and mathematical ratios, to make architectural structures with stellar correspondences. They are part of the plan for the return of the ancient civilization, and will become active when that time comes. They are anchors for planned reincarnation.

I develop a strong affinity with the head priest: our energies, bodies and thoughts are well aligned.

I trust him, I follow his instructions instinctively, and our collaboration yields many results. He doesn't speak much, and we communicate through other, more direct and precise channels. We know how to guide our emotions and channel our life force. Sexual magic, well prepared unions scheduled in the proper moments of time, functional to the project. Our body and spirit are purified. In these moments, the very matter of our flesh changes consistency: I touch the priest and I feel he's not completely solid.

I spend long hours in this place, and when I come back up, it's in the gardens that I regain contact with the beauty of the world. I'm happy and fulfilled, grateful to the gods for allowing me to be in my right place in the universe.

Suddenly, a huge roar shakes the laboratory. I am twenty-two years old; I die instantly under the collapse, together with the priest. With our last breath we intertwine our KAs and, united, we easily follow the path to the Beyond.

Many subtle helpers arrive, and the serpents that defended the laboratory now protect our passage. I know that the Goddess of divine justice Maat will be merciful. I'm curious to meet her.

THE MAN WHO SOARED IN THE SKY

Central America. Ancient civilization.

I love the beauty and harmony of my city so much! Perfect circles, terraces, water and gardens. Everything is bright and colorful under the sunlight. The gods designed it for us, the gods taught us how to build it. Not to us exactly, to our ancestors. The gods came flying. We must not forget that. It's me, and those like me, who help our people remember.

I don't know exactly where I was born; I've been living inside the temple compound since I can remember. I run and jump all the time; every task I'm given is an opportunity to test myself and train my body. I'm smaller than most of the other boys, but more agile and resilient.

I do everything willingly, but what I love most is taking care of the aviaries. They host large, brightly colored parrots with shiny feathers that adorn the headdresses of kings. They are sacred birds, and our priests care for them and revere them; only kings, dancers, and Flyers are granted the great honor of being connected to them, of wearing their feathers. And of all people, only the Flyers can become like them.

I know this is what I want to become. I'm not afraid. I know I can throw myself off the very high cliff held by a rope tied up only at one ankle. It's a difficult path, many give up during the training, I feel I'll make it; I won't stop in front of anything, neither the pain, nor the loneliness that purification imposes.

I'm accepted amidst the trainees that I am still a boy. I learn the sacred sounds of power to summon the forces of the air and start the flight. I learn the difficult secret breath that makes us soar up high in the air like the gods we represent, the gods we call inside our bodies. During the great celebrations of harvest and rebirth, through us the gods remind the people of the secrets of life, again and again. The priests observe and divine: by our movements and the duration of our flight they'll know what to expect from the coming season.

I spend much time with the sacred birds, observing and imitating them. I take drinks that open my senses and let me feel the gentle touch of their mind in mine; over time, I learn to move my consciousness into theirs. So, inside of them, I learn to fly, to follow the airstreams and dive down.

When I take my first jump with my physical human body, I am so intertwined with the mind and the senses of the birds, that the flight is just an exhilarating descent. It feels so natural! I hear the beating of the drums, the screaming of the people; I perceive the strong smell of burning herbs reaching the top of the mountain. I just look up at the sun, feel my body covered with the ritual feathers and leap into the void.

I wake up on my mat, long after the effects of the ritual drink I took have worn off. I'm so proud to have succeeded, to have earned my place within my people, that I pay no attention to the excruciating pain in my body. I know it will pass.

Many seasons go by, many celebrations. The damaging effects of the flights on my body are now permanent, together with the pain that never leaves me. My joints are out of alignment, a tremor runs through my limbs making it difficult to use my hands. I know it happens to all the Flyers: at a certain point our physical body is no longer the appropriate tool to soar in the sky with the gods. I know what I have to do—what we all do—because it's only to the air and its Forces that we belong.

Before diving one last time, I loosen the rope that's supposed to keep me well tied to the boulder at the top of the cliff. I know my ankle will slip out.

I carefully prepare my final flight. I purify myself; I adorn myself with special, very rare feathers and many jewels. I'm magnificent to behold, I will be resplendent even to the gods.

I jump with trepidation, anticipating the joy of passing into a new dimension. The impact is very strong, but I see only a great, wonderful light.

A WOMAN WHO WAS ALSO A MAN, AND A LIFE WORTH TWO

Thirteen century. Area of present-day Uzbekistan.

The constant hustle and bustle of my city, located at the crossroads of many trade routes, is the background music of my entire life. It makes me feel safe, protected. I don't like to move outside its walls, I feel that there are enemies and dangers everywhere. I'm the only heir of a wealthy merchant; my father is diplomatic and intelligent enough to win and keep the favor of the king and all levels of nobility. From a young age I see that my father's actions are not always entirely honest, but I understand that there's no other way. Politics are a dangerous game of favors and alliances and commerce depend on the support of the nobles.

My mother helps him in every way she knows how—and there are so many! Our wealth seems to never be enough to please her; perhaps it's because everyone tells her she's as beautiful as a queen. Unfortunately, her blood is not noble and she couldn't become one. As a young woman, however, she spent a few years in the king's harem and learned all the arts of a royal concubine. Precious secrets that hold great power, which she begins to teach me from an early age.

In me, my mother's beauty combines with my father's intelligence: I grow up into an attractive and self-confident woman. I love luxury and fine objects, but I'm not obsessed with wealth like my mother is. Rather, I want to become someone in my city; I want to have influence, power and freedom.

For years I follow my father everywhere. At first he objects saying that it's not proper for a woman, but nothing can steer me from my intention. Beyond my father's protests, I feel his pride in seeing me so strong and determined. I often have to disguise myself as a man and be introduced as his son. Playing with this double identity becomes my way of life. I feel I'm more complete if there are two me's, with different ideas and tastes. I have enough strength and will power for both of them: I do everything I can to let both of them express themselves and enjoy life.

I watch everything and everyone carefully, and learn to read the facial expressions of men of many different cultures. These differences fascinate me. I learn languages easily, and never show how much I understand, in order to have an advantage in negotiations. I decide that the woman-me speaks certain languages, the man others. I learn to fight and use a sword, as well as dance and enhance my beauty with makeup and fine dresses.

People close to me are confused by this, but I'm not. On the contrary, I feel more and more comfortable in this game of personalities: I'm very focused, and develop the art of doubles to perfection, so much so that many servants believe there are actually a daughter and a son, who was raised elsewhere for a few years.

I learn quickly everything my father has to teach, and I want to do more. As a man, I can go to all the meetings and hear the stories of the merchants from all over the world. As a woman, I can charm the caravan leaders into telling me the secrets of their routes. I study the maps and see the possibility of a different passage that would reduce the time necessary to travel to the plateau. I persuade my father to hire me as a business partner and finance my first expedition. He agrees on the condition that I don't go, neither as a woman nor as a man, because it's too dangerous.

I'm actually happy about this condition; even my male side doesn't like to leave the city without my father's protection. It's the right choice because a party of marauders attack the caravan and kill a few of our men. Fortunately the damage to the goods is contained, and for the following expedition to be a success, I only need to increase the armed escort.

Our wealth grows rapidly. I have a new wing of our palace built, with two different entrances and quarters, so that both me's can have their well separated spaces. I spend plenty of time at the baths to relax and think, and enjoy long massages with scented oils.

Many men ask for my hand in marriage, but I don't pay any attention to them: I need neither their protection nor their money. I hire as many as I need to advance my trade, and I give myself pleasure with the young men I choose and buy at the market. Of course, I conduct my negotiations dressed as a man, and that's already part of my enjoyment. They come from all over the world and are happy and grateful to be chosen for this role instead of as mere servants. It amuses me immensely to see their astonished expression when they discover my soft, scented body under my masculine clothes. When I get tired of their company, all I have to do is choose new ones. After a while, my male self also wants to participate fully in my love games, and so I choose women as well for my moments of play. The more time goes by, the more easily my body moves between the two characters—I don't even feel the difference.

My trades are increasingly successful, but I also feel the dangers around me escalating. When my father dies, his enemies become mine.

Greed, jealousy, and an unstable political situation create a myriad opportunities for betrayal. I rarely leave the palace, servants taste my food before I eat it, and everyone is searched upon entering. I have two guards at my side all the time, even when I'm sleeping.

Alas, the two me's are not in agreement on this policy. This is actually the man's decision, while the woman doesn't think it's necessary—she feels confined and unhappy. Their arguments in my head become loud and shrill, so much so that sometimes they don't even let me sleep. Maybe I should just choose one of the two, but I really don't know which part of me to give up.

I'm relaxing in the wonderful warm, scented water of the baths when a new argument starts in my head. I'm too tired to listen to the altercations of the two of them: I let my head gently slide under the water so that I don't hear their voices anymore. When I try to lift it up and breathe, a hand from above holds my head under the water. I panic for a moment, then realize that this life is worth two: if I die now, I won't have to give up any part of myself. I stop struggling and, finally, silence is all there is.

A LOOK THAT CALMED THE STORMS

Portugal. Renaissance.

My eyes. They say they are magnificent, the color of the sea after a storm, and they convey the same sense of calm. Looking at them, they say, all the inner storms subside, and the sun begins to shine in their heart again.

I've never seen my eyes. Just as I've never seen anything else. I was born like this, the first son of a rich merchant, the favorite trader of the local lord. Only my father can find him all these special fabrics and spices that come from beyond the great seas. My parents have neither the time nor the intention to take care of me, as they can hardly entrust their trade to a blind man. They prefer to pretend that I don't exist.

The Duke's wife, who has just had a baby, takes pity on me and decides to raise me with her son, so that he can have a playmate. When I grow older, she tells me that she'd sensed something special in me, she knew I'd be important for him.

This adoption of sorts is the greatest gift life can give me. Right away I become fond of my almost-brother, I perceive him as a part of me. I feel a distinct shiver on my skin when he's angry or hurt, and an exciting sensation of electricity when he's happy.

I experience the world as waves of light and warmth that my skin can read. I feel the boundaries of my physical body if I touch it, but my sensations extend much farther. My ears hear beyond sound, I often understand what people don't say; I sense their thoughts, I know what they hide in their hearts. Even the scent of objects has a light, a gentle current I feel flowing on my skin, telling me stories of the beauty of the world I live in and, more importantly, of the lives of the people around me. The presence of my almost-brother is the brightest of all in my heart.

He plays a stringed instrument, and I learn to sing. He has a talent for painting, and I can feel the quality of his work by sensing it with my fingers. He comes to me constantly to seek advice, for his art and his choices. My friend becomes a strong and enthusiastic young man, proud of his family and eager to live every experience in life to the fullest. I follow him in everything; when we are together I forget I'm different from the others.

We are inseparable. Love is born from our friendship, like a flower from its seed, like a lake from a mountain spring.

This feeling is the sweetest and deepest of all the currents I feel on my skin, in my mind, in my heart. He's full of passion and fire, and often has other lovers, men and women, but I'm not jealous. No one can experience his essence the way I do. We are the mirror of each other's souls.

When his father dies, he takes his place and our lives change. He marries quickly, the balance among the nobles is delicate, and he needs to have an heir right away. When I hold his son in my arms for the first time, I feel the strength of life coming, full of power and possibility. It's a miracle, a burst of joy that comes from Heaven to Earth. A feeling so deep pervades me that I know it's God's presence I'm sensing in that little creature.

A deep gratitude towards his mother makes my love for his father even stronger. The bond with this little one transforms me into a father as well. I'll be a loving and supportive presence in every choice of his life.

I'm appointed as the Duke's personal advisor, and I'm always by his side. We ride together to supervise the farmers working on his land; my heightened senses are often useful in ascertaining the truth and solving problems.

After the mystical experience I had holding the newborn in my arms, a new sensitivity opens up in me. I am certain that God exists: I see the light coming from high above to meet another light in the hearts of men and women, a brilliance that comes from the Earth. Only God can have created this wonder, so that the world of men may be rich in harmony and beauty. I pray and sing hymns to Him, and I feel his presence in my heart always.

Many years go by, as quick as the breeze that blows in autumn over the hills. The time comes when my lord gives his role to his son. We're old now, and I know that my days near him are over, my time among men is concluded. The silence and the welcoming darkness of a monastery welcome me. I spend my days in contemplation, my heart full of gratitude.

I die peacefully, during morning prayers. To follow the light, all I need now is my heart.

A WARRIOR WITH HANDS OF LIGHT

Coast of Turkey. Fortified city. Ancient times.

I was born into a proud and noble family. Our ancestors founded this city, a wonder that is a tribute to the glory of humans and gods. Gold and white create a special light that reflects in every space, making even the air soft and alive. I delight in the brilliance of the sun shining on the waves at sunset. I love every stone, every flower, every statue, every tiny piece of marble in my city. I enjoy the scent of its warm air, whose background note is the salty smell of the sea; I breathe it slowly, relishing and welcoming the power of nature entering my body. I feel happy, alive, and powerful.

I like to walk on the balcony of my family palace, one of the highest up in the walled city, just below the sacred area of the temples. No humans live above us, only the gods. It's the gods themselves that wanted our city to be built; ancient forces linked to the Sun and to Light: their splendor enlivens everything within and around us. Together with them, we weave the threads of our destiny; with the blessing and the touch of the Higher Forces we give birth to our children. There is a trace of their power in each of us; we're all well aware that we're a small people of semi-gods. For this reason, I never walk outside the city walls;

I'm not interested in what happens beyond them. I fear that if I left the magical bubble protecting our space, I would become an ordinary person. There could be no worse fate.

Art, wealth and beauty are not just around us for decoration or glory: they are the foundation of the energies that shape our thoughts, our dreams and even our appearance. Nothing is superfluous, or random. Everything has meaning: this is the essence of true magnificence.

Due to my noble rank I grow up with the royal princesses. We sing and weave, play wind and stringed instruments, and also train for combat, both hand-to-hand and with weapons. Just like the men, all the women of my people must be able to protect our sacred city.

I'm strong, tall, and agile. My hair is the color of light gold, like that of most of us. I have a fierce, fiery temperament. I really enjoy training and pushing my body and mind ever so slightly further and further, taking on new challenges that engage me to the fullest.

I'm afraid of nothing, and I fight better than many men. Most of them aren't even worthy of a glance from me. I am pure, noble, worthy of a God.

I don't feel the desire for a husband, and for my pleasure I carefully select my companions. They must be handsome and virtuous in spirit. The rest of my time I prefer to be in the company of women, whom I find more interesting and stimulating.

My hands have a special power: through them I can project a light that strikes like lightning. My training focuses on controlling this power. I must learn to harmonize the impulses of my temper, and modulate my strength, becoming aware of the feminine and masculine energies within me. I need to balance and integrate them so that I can be fully a woman.

Several years go by, and finally my instructors consider me ready. My task will be to make sure the shield of mystical energies around the city is always active, so that no discordant frequencies can go through it. My place of operation is inside the temple of the god of Light. I perceive the shield with my hands, and use the energy I've learned to emit and control to weave and reweave its web, and to repair holes if I find any. My life is fully centered on this, I have no room for a family and children. I'm proud I've found my rightful place.

The myths of our people tell of the deeds of our ancestors; they speak of their victories over the many attacks of enemies, horde after horde of them. So many died trying to climb our walls. No one ever succeeded in entering our city. Our gods have always been the most powerful, our priests know what to do. In our wonderful temples, our offerings to the gods never cease, all Forces connected to us are nurtured, and our golden bubble of protection has always remained intact.

I'm about twenty-five years old when a new attack comes. This new swarm of enemies is different from the previous ones: they are fiercer, more organized. I feel the baseness of their desires, how much they covet our gold. The color of their skin, their eyes, are so different from ours; their screams in the air send shivers down the spine of all of us. There are so many of them, moving like a huge animal running amok. I perceive the energy level of the forces connected to them, they are brutal, cruel and very powerful. I sense that they're also fed by the connected minds of many felines.

After many violent attacks, our enemies enter the city through a tunnel dug under the walls; we don't have enough force to push them back. Many of us die fighting, some save themselves by escaping by sea. They manage to salvage the temple's most sacred objects, so that our enemies will never even touch them.

The city's protective energy bubble is destroyed. When I realize there’s nothing left to repair, I throw myself into the sword fight. I’m exhausted, and I know I won’t last long, but I will die with honor, together with my people. Our name will be remembered forever, and the wrath of our gods will punish our enemies.

A SECRET AGENT AS FAST AS THE WIND
Vietnam. Fifteenth century. Reign of the Emperor Lê Thái Tông.

I move light and fast. The large leaves of the trees envelop me; the tapping of the rain muffles the noise of my movements. I've been watching the geckos since I was a child and, little by little, they shared their secrets with me. Now I can climb walls and roofs, trees and stairs just like them. The earth doesn't bind me the way it does to others: it's partially my training, partially a gift of life.

I was born into a large, happy and peaceful family of humble origins. For generations everyone has worked in the rice fields; we share our home with many relatives. My mother sings all the time, my father smiles and prays. Our simple hut is always permeated by the scent of resins offered to the ancestors mixed with the smell of moldy wood and boiled rice. I love this place, but I know staying here is not my destiny. I'm full of dreams and energy; eager to discover what lies beyond the rice fields, far beyond the forest.

Men dressed in beautiful clothes pass by the village from time to time to collect taxes, and I'm always the first to run out to watch them. I'm not afraid of them, nor of their tall horses: I am enchanted and impressed by their majestic and powerful appearance, and dream of being like them one day.

I've just turned fifteen when everyone starts talking about the new times that have come: the Emperor is changing the world, protecting our country and giving every man with a noble soul a chance to become somebody! I feel this is the perfect time for me, and I decide to finally find out what fate can offer me.

The wise master of our ancient fighting arts accepts me as one of his disciples. He's young and energetic, and I admire him greatly. I learn to read, sit in contemplation, keep silent and obey. I learn to control fear and focus my thoughts. Concentration becomes the power allowing me to move as if I were flying. The sense of euphoria I feel when I run as fast as the wind makes me feel invincible. I learn to fight with one stick and then with two; with one sword and then with two, but it's my own body, the most powerful weapon.

War breaks out in the north of our country. I'm a healthy and strong young man, agile and well-trained, ready to join the army. I leave with my father's blessing; my mother and brothers hug me with such love and emotion that I'm sure the memory of their embrace will last forever, to give me comfort in case of need.

I am so excited! During the long walk north, many other young men join our contingent; the leaders watch us, test us, select us. Each task we're given is a way to assess our courage, our focus, and our skills. By the time we get to the army headquarters, I've already been chosen to join a special unit for covert operations. The training is so hard that sometimes I can't hold back the tears streaming down my face. But, through the effort and pain, I feel my body and mind reach new levels of mastery, day after day, hour after hour, minute after minute. My relationship with time changes: I start to perceive it within me and learn to slow it down and stretch it at will. I learn to jump so high I can almost fly; to fight blindfolded; to expand my senses and perceptions to the maximum. I learn to sleep with my eyes open; to read people's expressions and movements, and predict their actions and thoughts. I discover the full power of the human body.

I'm on a small team of three agents. We're given special tasks—always secret, always dangerous. We don't live near each other, and for our protection we are given false identities and jobs. I am, officially, the owner of a small spice store.

My employees are all spies: we hear so much useful information from people chatting away while shopping...

I only get together with the other two agents at the times of our missions; we protect each other and know our lives depend on each other. We're aware that we work for the Emperor, and even though we never meet him, this gives us great pride; we are confident that everything we do is in the highest service of our country.

I'm required to not have a family. It doesn't seem like much of a sacrifice, I think the love for my people and my country will be enough to keep my heart happy... until the day I fall madly in love. It's a fire I can't control; I run to see my beloved whenever I can, even though I've been warned that I mustn't. Holding her in my arms gives a new flavor to my life, a new scent to my dreams. I'm sure I'll find a way to have her by my side forever; a way to make everything work out.

One day I find her room empty, and no one can tell me where she went. I feel so guilty and desperate that I'd like to drop everything and go looking for her, even on the moon. But I know that I wouldn't stay alive for more than a minute, so I hide my pain, and never talk about it with anyone.

I continue to look for her secretly for the rest of my life.

She becomes a companion that helps me transform and open my soul, a presence always nudging me towards the higher values I have within. Sometimes, I meet other women that remind me of her: the color of her eyes, the shininess of her hair, the lightness of her skin—sometimes even the same tone of voice... Small details that help me keep her alive in me, and ease my pain.

I live a long life. When my body loses its agility, I move to a small hut in the heart of the forest, where my work in the service of the Emperor continues. Many young men are brought to me, to be trained and turned into agents. I can see right into their souls: I start instructing them only if I perceive honor and virtue.

I feel death approaching. I'm thankful that it didn't take me through a weapon, or in my sleep, but invited me to be present for the most important moment of my life. I die on a beautiful misty morning that smells of grass and sky—after my usual cup of tea, the greatest pleasure of my day. I hope that, wherever I'm going, I can finally be reunited with my beloved. If she's not there yet, I'll wait for her.

A CARAVAN LEADER DRESSED IN RED

Northern Asia. Mountains. Nineteenth century.

Prayer flags waving in the air like notes of a chant to the gods. The plateau is green and fragrant; the wind plays with the grass, and I run happily breathing deeply. My mother loves red in all shades, and in our family we wear the most vibrant clothes of all. Even our nicknames are linked to this color, and I'm proud of it. Red suits my temperament: I have great energy, joy of living, and I'm curious about everything.

The infinite sky, the slow walk of our animals, the cries of the men returning to the village, the song of the women during their thousand daily chores: I like it all. Everything resonates within me like a love song to life. And thus, I sing too, finding the right tune for each of my daily tasks by slightly changing our traditional songs. Nothing feels hard to me in my day, which begins at dawn with prayers and the scent of incense filling every corner of our comfortable tent.

I have great love and admiration for my older brother, and whenever I can, I follow him like a shadow. He laughs and doesn't give me much consideration: he treats me with affection, a little bit as if I were a pet. I watch everything he does,

I learn everything: how to load horses and yaks with goods in the right way; how to prepare the supplies; how to determine who will carry out all the different tasks during the journey.

I'm still a girl, but I've already decided: I'm going to join a caravan, too. It's not a traditional role for a woman, but I don't care. I prepare for years, venturing away from the camp alone further and further to discover the paths that men follow, asking questions of everyone I meet on the way... I persuade my brother to teach me how to ride; the communication with the horse is instinctive, easy, it feels like a flow of energy intertwining with mine.

My family starts talking about marriage for my older sisters; I know my turn will come next, I need to accelerate my moves... My brother is getting ready to leave again with his group: the night before his departure I take his yak and set off along the path I know they will follow. I leave clues for him, so that he won't be alarmed. He catches up with me; he's angry but also very amused.... I beg him to let me stay; he accepts convinced that the hardship of the journey will make me soon run home.

And it's really a challenge, but the beauty of my land, the majesty of the sky, the sense of freedom opening my heart and soul are stronger than all obstacles. I'm sure this is the life I want.

On the way back I sneak off from the group just before arriving at our village. I have my share of goods and a horse with a large necklace of red beads in its mane. It's a good luck charm, like the locket I wear around my neck. I know my family will cry and my heart is sad, but I won't be free to leave again if I go back home. I pray as I walk away, scared and excited at the same time.

The first months are really difficult. I'm accepted into caravans where they make me work as a servant. I often have to protect myself from the men, especially at night. I learn from every experience, and become very skilled at using a knife. I feel more and more secure, and the men start treating me with greater respect.

Long journeys. Dawns of every color. Prayers, and sound of prayer wheels in the wind; the sacred shelter of the monasteries in the blizzards... My body changes, becomes stronger and more agile, my skin hardens with the sun and the wind. I sing and shout my presence to the sky. I go back to my village a few times, my heart fills with joy seeing the places of my childhood, finding the warm affection of my family.

On the altar at home I make offerings to the Spirits to thank them for their gifts, and pray to them to keep everyone healthy.

My brother becomes the head of the caravan and agrees to take me along. Now I can sleep peacefully, there's no need to embrace my dagger. The man sleeping next to me is a childhood friend: our love is a shared life of freedom, determination and joy. I have a daughter who moves with me tied up to my body; she breathes with me the wind and dust of our highlands, the infinite beauty of our sky. I know that life in a caravan is not suitable for a child, so she'll grow up in the village with my family, but in these first years I want her all to myself.

I die on my way back from the village, after leaving my daughter there. My heart is heavy and tears blur my vision. To gain strength, I put my hand on my belly and feel the new life growing inside me. The wind blows hard, a sudden wave of dust hits me and the reins slip out of my grip. The horse stumbles, we lose our bearings.

I fly off the cliff, then I feel I'm soaring higher and higher. Beyond the dust I see an immense sky, so golden and bright like never before.

A MASAI ON THE PLATEAU

Kenya. Seventeenth century.

My eyes see as far as the land extends. I can make out the silhouette of our cattle from so far away that to everyone else they're just dark dots on the red earth. I see all the bushes, the birds, the lizards. My father says I need to pair my extraordinary sight of outside things, with my sight of inner ones, so that I can become a good leader.

My father is powerful and respected. I know my place and I'm willing to do whatever it takes to be worthy of it, to deserve the name my father gave me. It's an ancient and glorious name, chosen a week before I was born, when my father felt the soul that was coming could make me a valiant warrior.

My family owns a large herd of cattle, and I grow up with a baby calf, as if he were my brother. I paint his body and mine with ochre, the same color of our land, a tribute to our mother earth. I learn that water is also sacred, I need to know how to protect and preserve it. My mother is proud of me, she colors my scalp and combs my hair into very elaborate hairstyles, to remind me of who I am. My body is strong, well trained, tall and agile.

I run fast, always keeping my spear by my side. I feel it's an extension of me. My body is decorated with cuts and tattoos, showing my name. Together with the other young men—as eager as I am to embark on hunts and challenges—every day I seek out new territories. I must prove that I'm useful to the people.

All my age transitions are marked by specific and secret rituals: already as a boy, my initiations give me more and more power and understanding. I learn to face my fears, to endure pain, to dance with the other warriors. I pray to the God Enkai to let me always hear his song in my heart, and have power in my body to bring it to life with movement. I learn what loyalty is.

My greatest test is to take the life of the mighty lion. I know I can only do this if he chooses me, if he agrees to give me his energy in exchange for something greater for his people and mine. This is a pact as ancient as life, an exchange of essences for the balance of the Whole. I purify and prepare, aware that if no lion will accept me, mine will be the life I must offer to the Earth.

The search is long, one after the other I face fears I never thought I had. I focus on each moment I'm living as if it were the only one; I savor every drop of the precious little water I have with me as if it could give me all the energy of the lake; I observe and touch my spear until I feel it coming alive with my own will. Then I meet the lion.

I perceive his smell, then I hear his contained roar, to which I respond with my own voice, low and without tremor. One leap, and my spear strikes him in the heart. The thud of his mighty body falling startles me, as if the whole hunt had been a dream. I succeeded in killing him without making him suffer, and I'm immensely grateful for this.

I feel I'm one with life now; the legacy of my people is fully awake in my blood. I protect our people's livestock from several attacks, and participate in raids to steal livestock from other tribes.

I am brave and swift, I listen to the wind and the sun and know when it's time to attack. I'm skilled at tracking and smelling the various prey we hunt.

I feel very powerful in the group of men, we all move as one single body. We're splendid to behold, a group of proud warriors, colorfully dressed, dancing with the power to connect heaven and earth for the glory of Enkai.

As the seasons pass, I conquer beaded necklaces to add around my neck, as well as bracelets for my wrists and ankles. My goal is to acquire as many of them as possible to prove my worth as a warrior. I mix the colors of my clan with the messages I want to share with others: loyalty, strength, the beauty of life reflected in the thousand shades of the colors of our God.

I can remain still for a long time, and I often spend long periods on the plateau as a sentinel. I feel I lose myself in the vastness of space; my senses expand and I often perceive atmospheric changes long before they take place. Suddenly, new people start walking on the plateau: sad steps, tears and pain. I'm one of the first to see them.

I lead my companions on the high path, and what we see fills our hearts with horror. Men with faces of a different color, in sad clothes, drag the people of our land in a long caravan of chains and violence. Men, women and children. It never seems to end...

They're still far from the land of my people, but my soul freezes with terror. I look at my beautiful wives, my many happy children, all the other people and our animals: I feel so much love for them all, and a great anger at what we've seen.

With the other warriors, I ritually offer some of our blood to God, vowing that we'll never let this happen to our people. From that moment on, our fiercest and most powerful warriors patrol the plateau.

When the caravans get too close to our sacred paths, we attack. Often the despicable pale-faced men are so frightened at the mere sight of us that they flee and abandon that route. I lead many expeditions and many attacks and we win all the time, but more of them keep returning. I have dark dreams of what's to come.

I die of an infection, from a fighting wound. I'm surrounded by my family and all the people pray for me, performing the rituals for my passing.

My last action is to look into the eyes of my eldest son. I want to pass on to him my wisdom and experience, as well as a vision of strength and hope for the future. I know my people will need it.

A WOMAN IN THE TEMPLE OF DOLPHINS

Ancient empire of Mu. Pacific Ocean. About 40,000 years ago.

I don't like to go to the surface much. Most of my life takes place underwater. I was born inside one of the large illuminated bubbles protected by the Feminine Forces of water, in an area of the ocean considered sacred by the whole people. These Powers preside over the flows that create the safe routes throughout the marine world, the protected pathways for travel and the areas of contact with different species.

In my genetic code there are traits of a human race much older than most surface humans. I still have DNA segments of a very advanced and intelligent marine species, similar to large octopuses. They lived in this ocean a long time ago, before reaching such a high level of complexity that they could transcend dimensions, and move to a higher vibrational frequency than planet Earth has in this epoch.

My code doesn't appear so much in my physical body—even though my head is larger than that of surface humans, and my skin much thicker. Above all, I have an extraordinary memory and the ability to detect every slightest change in the pressure, flows and temperature of the sea.

Small openings behind my ears and along my neck allow me to sense the environment. My lung capacity is very high, and I can spend a lot of time underwater without having to activate oxygen bubbles for breathing. My eyesight perceives many shapes and shades, even in the absence of light.

But perhaps, what sets me apart most from surface humans is the level of empathy and connection I have with marine animals and my people. There are only a few thousands of us left, and for the most part we all still live underwater. In the past few generations more and more of us have chosen to change their genetic programming to live on the surface.

With a part of me I sense them all—it's a network of connection that makes us strong and coordinated. We rarely have disharmonious emotions; we are mature and present from childhood, and the wisdom of our species is passed on to us by osmosis, rather than through study. By natural predisposition, we work closely with the dolphins in charge of water surveillance, both to prevent possible natural disasters and attacks at the borders. They're unlikely, but not impossible.

Communicating empathically with the cetaceans has been very natural for me since I was a child.

I study all their transmission frequencies; I learn the sound signals that I reproduce with a special instrument, and I communicate far beyond mere technical exchanges. I learn to modulate emotional sequences, which make me welcome and appreciated. I'm often the officer called by the Governors of the Kingdom to translate their messages, and negotiate the renewal of pacts with these highly evolved, ancient dwellers of the ocean.

One of the most extraordinary moments of my life is when I'm admitted inside one of the temples of the Divine Forces of Dolphins. It's not a physical place, but a vibrational space that allows contact with the Mind of Dolphins on all planets in our part of the galaxy. I can hardly believe I've been granted this honor.

The dolphins accompany me beyond dimensions following the movement of an energy spiral, but when I reach its center I'm completely alone. Only in this way can I feel the Whole. I have the sensation of exploding into billions of fragments of light, and morphing into an immense web of radiance and connection. For a time that seems infinite, I lose all identity to become one with evolution, with the Matrix of Life, with the divine Program in the universe.

This experience touches and changes me deeply. I choose to embrace a monastic path. I continue my work serving the community, but I move to an area on the side of an underwater temple. I study and I serve. I become a Guardian of the Gateway to a very high divine dimension, nurturing the Forces that keep our space-time cohesive.

I live a very long life, and as time passes, the traits of my marine code become more pronounced. Along with my body, my mind changes, and I feel more and more connected to the Program that will bring us back to being one, cohesive, conscious divine emanation.

In accordance with my monastic status, I don't choose the programming of my rebirth, but entrust it to the higher priests.

My death is a conscious transition. The sound frequencies of the dolphins open a Door for me; I feel myself melting inside one of the great crystals of the temple. A part of my memories and perceptions will remain there forever, while my essence reunites with the Flow of the Whole.

A SOLDIER WHO EMBRACED A REVOLUTION

France. Second half of the eighteenth century.

Loyalty has been my main characteristic since childhood, even when the other boys made fun of me because I was willing to lose everything rather than betray my playmates. As an adult, this trait becomes a kind of inner compass guiding my actions and choices; and it's often challenged by the confusion and violence around me.

I was born into a family of merchants, in the countryside not far from the King's magnificent residence. My parents die when I am still a child. They leave their business to my uncles who, in exchange, promise to take care of me. I rarely lack food or clothing, but I never feel loved or welcome in their home. They have other children, lots of work and many worries. Rumors from the city speak of hunger and desperate situations. We work for the court and things here still seem rather normal: everything is submitted to the needs of the King and his nobles, who continue to inundate us with orders and requests. Louis XVI is the point of reference for our entire community: he's King by divine right, and everyone is proud to serve him.

Then, almost suddenly, things change drastically for us, too.

The nobles of the court, who always make us wait for our due, stop paying altogether. There's despair, discontent, tension and many begin to criticize the King. On the contrary, I think our Monarch is noble and great, he cannot be the one responsible for these injustices, there must be other reasons. My loyalty makes my heart fly up to the sky of France, to embrace all of my homeland: as soon as I am old enough to be accepted, I'll join the royal army. I know that I'll never become an officer—that's only for the nobles—but I think serving as an infantryman is just as honorable.

The army is not the orderly, safe world I expected. Luckily, my natural optimism, my wish to make myself useful and give meaning to my life sustain me even in the most confusing times. Or maybe they keep me from realizing how bad things really are. I'm respectful of superiors, and resourceful enough to find solutions the many times their commands don't seem to come, or are confusing and contradictory.

I train with focus and presence, and become very proficient in the use of all the weapons provided. I'm a point of reference for others. My garrison is stationed in the area where I was born, so we are among the first to be called up to provide security for the King and his court during the Estates-General.

When I see the palace up close—and even more so when I'm admitted inside—I remain as if paralyzed in a state of great awe, for a long time. The beauty, the gold, the myriad reflections of the light on the huge, gilded mirrors deeply touch my soul, as if they were symbols of a world of perfection that perhaps really exists somewhere else. But I have no time to look for it, not even in my dreams.

The tension and fear in the air, the new ideas circulating and reaching us confuse me, and raise new questions in my mind and heart. Soldiers begin to steam up, and many flare with wrath. I believe changes can take place peacefully, that new values can transform the excesses and injustices that are now so obvious before my eyes.

I'm one of the soldiers sent to Paris to counter the July Revolution. Nothing could have prepared me for the horror of what I encounter. What I saw there haunts me in my sleep; it's in front of my eyes every minute of my day. Also my heart and soul seemed to get lost in the red of the blood that was everywhere. Screaming, smoke, malnourished and mangled men, women and children, their eyes alive with a fire I've never seen before, fighting on barricades with rocks and pitchforks, slings and sticks, blocking passage to the city.

There are flames all around their blockades, and they look like terrifying demons straight out of hell. We have no precise orders. The army hesitates; we're stuck in a strange limbo, until the order to retreat comes. The officers, who are all nobles, are beginning to desert: the army is like a huge crazed animal that moves without direction or objective, driven by fear and in great confusion.

The new ideas are now everywhere, they seem to have a power giving them life; they touch and ignite hearts; they carry the vision of a new future and voices coming from the other side of the world, demonstrating that equality and freedom are indeed possible. I wonder what to be loyal to, what is really important.

It causes me a lot of pain to have to admit that the King is not the hero I've adored all my life. This disappointment makes me feel more lost than the army's disbandment. Then I realize that, even without a battalion, I am still a soldier: of that I'm sure. And as a soldier I decide to do my part to build a new France.

I join the city militia. Thanks to my experience I'm entrusted with a command role. This is more than I ever dreamed of! Several of my comrades join me, so I have a group of loyal soldiers I trust completely: in these times, this is the rarest and most valuable thing.

The next three years are so intense that they seem to go by in an instant: hopes and victories, horrors and blood, exaltation and fear, a constant swing of extremes. I have no time to think; I live every moment knowing it could be my last. I tell myself that I'm in the right place; this violence is an indispensable, painful passage to end all tyrannies. I sleep little and eat even less, yet my body is strong and full of energy. In my soul, though, I feel much older than my years.

There are many women fighting with us. They are free, strong and passionate. Whenever possible, we share fleeting moments of sweetness and almost wild love before returning to the fight. These ardent exchanges are also part of the collective fever bringing us together and giving us strength to continue. This is not the time to think about a family and children, there is still too much screaming, too much hunger, so much pain around me—I never fantasize about anything for me beyond the present moment.

A bayonet shot hits my left leg, and the bleeding can't be stopped. I have no pain, I just feel more and more tired.

The noises around me become more and more distant, and I finally find a calm space in my heart, like a clean white sheet of paper, without even a stain of blood.

I take stock of my life, and pray to God that my actions—even the most violent ones—may be part of His plan for true justice among men.

I'm not twenty years old yet.

A WOMAN SOWING SEEDS IN TIME

Great Britain. Very ancient era.

The forest is my mother, my home, an extension of me. I was born near its water, the magical pond in the thick of the woods, where the sun comes through the leaves only at the height of day. A sunbeam touched my forehead at birth. It was a sign, my people said. It indicated I'm a special child, and I have a special task.

My mother is beautiful, strong and cheerful, like all the women of my people. It's the women who lead my people, and make sure that everyone can enjoy the gifts of the forest and life in a fair way. My father is not here; they say he's come and gone like a late summer wind. I find him in all the men of the tribe, as they all protect and love me.

Playing, I learn to recognize the herbs, the fruits and the roots. I have a healing touch, as many of us do. If I hold small wounded animals, they feel better; if I send thoughts of love to plants they grow stronger. The energy of life flows through me, coming from the sacred place underground, from the great crystal under the rocks.

I feel its presence in my mind, it's a secret access to a network of light, a passage to other worlds.

Maybe my father came from there? In dreams, I receive images and instructions; my mind seems to get in touch with many different places, places I've never seen, and that are very different from my forest. I feel all I have to do is let the images permeate me, give them time to show me what to do. Each of us has a task in life: I trust dreams will tell me mine.

I don't talk much; I don't touch others much. I grow up spending more time with the forest animals than with the other girls. Little by little the information I'm waiting for comes to my mind in flashes of light, showing me the way. I will have a daughter, but she won't be born here. I'm to get away from the forest. And find her father.

The memories of my people must take root in a new genetic line. Everything is changing, our gods are weakening. Lest we be lost in the lines of future, we must bring our seeds into beings connected to the new soul of time. I know what I need to do. I take off with the blessing of the elders. My peers help me get ready and dress me in the most beautiful of our robes. They put flowers in my long hair, and I wear inlaid wooden jewelry.

I walk slowly along the path at the edge of the forest until I hear a group of soldiers approaching.

They ride quickly, but stop when they see me. Surprised and fascinated, they agree to take me to the large stone-built house. I extend my consciousness to let my people know I'm safe, and leave with the soldiers.

I am greeted by two elderly women. I have the impression they've been waiting for me, but we don't exchange any comments. They feed me, and replace the flowers in my hair with glittering stones. I know the lord of the castle is to be the father of my child, and I'm ready to meet him.

He's young and arrogant, so different from the sweet-tempered men of my people. I feel his desire when he sees me, mixed with a sense of reverence. He never met a woman like me before. I create a shield with my mind to protect my energy field from his rougher traits, but I'm immediately drawn to him, too. It's as if we were both enraptured by a spell. I become his partner without even needing to discuss it. I'm amazed at how intrigued I am by his passion and love that is so physical and direct. His way of being and feeling is so different from mine, and it opens up new sensations in me.

I transform and channel his masculine energy. I use it to strengthen my spiritual communication with my people, to whom I send information through the wind and the special openings at the full moon. I become indispensable to him; he cannot stay away from me for long. He wants me to be at his side in his war councils and in all meetings. His mind and heart become an open field for me: I respect his honesty, his courage and the devotion he has for his people. I learn a lot from him about human drives and the art of government. He also teaches me how to fight so I can defend myself in case of attack, and I become very skilled with the sword.

I keep myself healthy with the herbs I gather and the waters I prepare in the different lunar cycles, and when the time is right I give birth to my daughter, a wonderful being of flesh and light. Our mental connection is complete, yet I feel her vibration is denser than mine. She will bring our seed closer to this plane; she will keep our memories alive in her body and that of her daughters. Through her, we'll take root in the new age that is beginning, and where there is no place for us. Her father also feels she's a special child, and treats her with love and devotion. I know he would give his life to protect her.

My daughter is about six years old when I start having alarming dreams. I see enemies coming from the North, storming through the forest and destroying my village. I send messages to my people to prepare for these terrible events, and I choose to return to fight with them. I leave the castle on a moonlit night, through the underground tunnels, and reach the forest.

By the time the enemies arrive, most of us have already fled into the thick of the woods in a different direction. I stay back to fight with my sword and my mind. These men have such a low vibration that I don't feel much humanity in them. I connect to the crystal energy underground and create a defensive net around the village.

I feel the earth shake, the village is on fire, but the access to the crystal is protected by the crumbling earth. No one will find it, and once the invaders are gone, my people will return. At least for a little while, before the next horde arrives. This, too, I see in the lines of time.

I die of a heart attack, releasing one last, powerful radiation of light against our enemies. My daughter is sleeping safely at the castle: I leave my body satisfied of having completed my most important task.

THUNDERING ROCK THE HUNTER

America. Great Plains. Before the arrival of the Europeans.

Inuna-Ina: our people. My people. I feel free among them; a son of this immense sky and this powerful land, on which we move following the eternal rhythm of the seasons. We are one single breath of the Great Spirit; we move as one; we live as one.

There's a place, a time and a role for everything. We, the men, are the warriors and the hunters; we protect and feed our people; we guard the ways of the ancestors, the ways the people of the stars taught them. Our women prepare the food; protect water and fire; build the tepees with buffalo hides. The buffalo giving us life, and that we follow across the plateau from season to season.

The women tell the stories of our ancestors in the quilts we wear with pride, or that we use to decorate our dwellings. Their hands create a beauty that competes with that of the world around us, rich in the colors of our lives, the sun, the grass, the snow and the water. Our women dance and sing in circles around us, while we, the men, reenact our bravest feats in the center around the fire; we follow the beat of the drum, becoming the rhythm of everyone's heart, until the night is over.

I know what my role will be for my people already as a child: my keen eyesight, my strong and fast body and my calm determination contain the promise of a hunter. I train to run as fast as the wind as I shoot my tomahawk and arrows, following their movements with my eyes. I learn to make my own arrows as a child—like we all do. I like to sit and feel the wood in my hands. I sing as I cut it, and my songs become more and more powerful as I grow up. It's a medicine I learn to master, the power of the breath coming out of my body and turning into a direction for my actions, into an effect for my intentions.

I know how precious the breath of life is, and I don't waste it on many words. I can hold it for a long time. I keep the air within me, let it travel to every part of my body while nothing in me moves. In this way, I become one with the trees, the sky, the air around me. Motionless and completely alert. A presence. Just a presence. Like an ancient rock.

Then, in an instant I run, following the path my eyes opened for me, so fast that I make everyone wince. It’s in this way that, through many tests, over time I gain the name I heard during my quest: Thundering rock that flies suddenly. I am firm and stable like a rock, but just like thunder I can strike with great power and speed.

My first encounters with the sacred buffaloes are the greatest thrill of my life: I never felt the power of the Creator so strongly before. The din of their running stirs something in my blood; I feel one with them, with the other men running with me, I'm aware this is the most sacred dance of life. Spirits are all around us, watching with how much honor and courage we take the lives of these powerful ancient beings.

I participate in the great ceremonies to honor the Sun and the Earth. With prayers and sweat I prepare and purify myself, and then I dance without stopping for a very long time. I offer my breath and my songs to feel one with the universe and contribute in regenerating the creative force of life. I never feel the need to offer the suffering of my body to transcend the physical dimension.

I gather wisdom as time passes, listening and listening. In the ceremonies I pay attention to the spirits; in the hunts to the birds, the wind, the grass; at the village to the conversations of the women. I listen to the voices of the elders and those of the children. I speak only when I think it's really useful.

My wives learn to understand me without words; their presence on my blanket at night is a sweet feeling that comforts me and allows me to rest deeply. Often, I meet wise spirits in my dream world. My children are a joy, and my gift to my people.

I become a member of the Council, sitting with the sage elders. I feel honored and ready to serve. I measure my words even more, feeling the power of each breath uttered on the sacred Pipe.

I die old, wearing my most precious and beautiful deer skins, and all my insignia. I'm ready, I knew the moment of passage was coming: I dreamed of a beautiful and powerful buffalo. It's time to run after it in the sacred prairies. It's winter, we are all at the camp.

I hear the cheerful voices of the men betting and playing, the songs of the women, the cries of the children: my heart is full of love and gratitude to the Great Spirit for all of them.

THE PROPHECY OF THE CRESCENT MOON

Very ancient era. Northern Greece.

I'm a woman and my birth is celebrated with joy. My mother is a young warrior. Her laughter is contagious, and her arms are strong and powerful. She doesn't lull me much; rather, from a young age she trains me with love and attention. I learn to fight while starting to walk and talk. It's our way to play, forge our character, and show our courage and determination. I'm never alone; there are many other girls in the group, and all the women give us attention and knowledge. I learn to recognize berries and roots to eat, and to hunt with a sling and arrows. I have a sixth sense that allows me to foresee danger: I often save the lives of my companions.

We are an ancient and strong tribe. Our myths tell us that we've been living in these forests, on these mountains, since the time of the ancient gods. The Moon Goddess herself was our first queen. Here, she met the Fire God who taught her to hunt. The Goddess asks us to respect the gift of life in every being, and take only what we need, nothing more. We help animals when they suffer; we protect the nature spirits of the forest and the water nymphs; we listen to the whispers of the wind and the earth.

We feed only on beings who've lived free until the moment they give their life to us. We don't eat anything unless it offers itself to our bows, or it's given to us spontaneously by the earth. We feel part of the Mother, we honor her with offerings and ceremonies, and she gives us strong daughters and many animals to hunt.

My active role for my people begins with my first blood cycle. From the Queen I receive a bow and arrows. It's a recognition of the role chosen for me: I'll be a warrior and a hunter for the good and prosperity of us all. I'm happy with this choice: I'm fearless and I love the freedom and the feeling of strength and energy that riding, running and hunting give me. To sanction the beginning of my new life, I kneel down and my mother marks the sacred sign of the moon on my forehead. When the hot iron touches me I feel a great pain, but I don't let a single moan escape my mouth.

Our tents are warm, cozy, full of hides and furs. There's always fresh water in the water-skins, and herbal drinks to replenish our body and quiet our mind. We wear metal and bone ornaments. We groom each other's long hair. We're tall, strong, beautiful and brave. Nothing scares us. We live each moment with passion. All the important tasks of life are performed by women.

We hunt, lead the people, fight the tribes of the low lands, deliver babies, offer sacrifices to the Goddess. We live each moment with intensity. There's much love, tenderness and care among us, trust and deep bonds.

Ancient rites of water and blood dedicated to the Moon. In the annual ceremonies in which we celebrate the meeting of the solar masculine force with the feminine within us, we choose the most handsome and strongest men among those the other tribes send us as a tribute. The nights of the ritual are illuminated by the full moon, the sound of the drums continues until dawn, and we all dance and unite our bodies around a large bonfire.

Some men leave immediately after the ritual, others stay with us for a while, in a special place where they forge metals and create tools, far from the sacred heart of our camp.

I have two sons, both healthy and strong. I entrust them to a neighboring tribe to be raised with the men. Their fate is not connected to mine. The third pregnancy is finally the daughter I've been waiting for. She has a small, half-moon-shaped birthmark on her forehead, with a dot on the side, as if it were a star.

It's a rare and precise identification mark, like that of our First Queen. Perhaps it's She who returns? An ancient prophecy says that when She comes back, a cycle will be completed, the stars will stop shining, and the Gates of the Beyond will open.

It's a dark prediction, disturbing, and not even the elders know much about it. I ask the moon, the water and the forest and, little by little, in my dreams I begin to understand its meaning: the time left to our people, in this forest, won't be long. Violent tribes are advancing towards us, fighting with weapons stronger than ours. We are brave and skillful, but the enemies are now many. They are hungry for more land, more animals to hunt. I hear in my dreams the screams of the forest as these men walk through it with heavy feet and threatening thoughts. Their minds are as dark as the winter mud at the bottom of a pond.

I share my visions with the Council and many share similar feelings. We discuss what to do. Some say it's time to leave; others want to stay, fight and try to hold back the invaders. The Queen and the elders tell us their decision: they saw each of us melt into a tree in the forest and turn into a bright light. We won't leave this land: even if we won't stop the invaders, we must try to.

We're a part of the forest, we can't thrive anywhere else. Our spirits will join the trees and through them we will live forever.

Our shamans arrange for the right connection rituals, evoke our ancestors, summon the tree spirits, and they accept the pact. The intertwining of our human essence with that of the vegetation will be a call for the Goddess, and she'll give us a new life in Her world. All we need is enough time to complete the magical ring around the forest and the ritual to unite our human souls with those of the trees.

The healers prepare an infusion to help the elderly, the little girls and the weaker women move gently and painlessly from the dream world into their chosen tree. The men who are at the camp can choose to leave, or tie their fate to ours. Most decide to go, and I know that this choice, too, is part of the design.

When everything is ready, I participate with my sisters in numerous fights to slow down the arrival of the invaders. Whoever of us dies now will immediatly melt their essence into a tree and continue to live. Little by little we'll all join them. I leave with my companions for my last battle. I have no fear.

A MERCHANT EVERYONE THOUGHT WAS A KING
Giordania, 100 a.C.

I was born into a wealthy family of traders. Already as a child, I accompany my father on his travels. I learn everything quickly and I'm still very young when I take off with my own caravan. I'm curious about all strange objects, the ones coming from far away, that tell stories I've never heard. All the other merchants know I buy them at a good price, and they always bring many to me. I choose the ones that strike me for their beauty as well as those that, by touching them, give me the impression of being clues to what I'm looking for.

I don't know exactly what it is, but I have a feeling that I have to wait for something, something different from what I have in my life now. And waiting isn't easy for me at all; I'm a man of action and this strange sensation gives me anxiety and fear. That's why I'm constantly on the move.

I don't care much about my work, but the less attention I pay to it the richer I become. I have many camels, rugs and precious objects. My tent looks like that of a prince, and just like a prince I dress. I wear rich robes, my beard is long and well groomed, as black as my eyes. I know I'm considered a handsome man—but also detached and cold.

My constant inner turmoil makes me feel separate from others. I often feel like they don't exist, and none of the activities of my life seem as important to me as this calling I cannot understand.

I don't know where this deep sense of longing comes from. I spend many sleepless nights. Only one song, always the same, manages to soothe my soul. It's an ancient chant of the desert; my wives and concubines sing it for me for hours on end. I have many beautiful women, from all the lands around us. Not even in them do I find the water that quenches the fire burning inside me.

One day my inner calling is so strong that I decide to set out alone towards the sea of salt. I spend three days and three nights without eating or sleeping; I am possessed by a strange feeling of excitement; I get flashes of visions and dreams that seem to indicate a precise route.

I reach an area rich in water and vegetation, and I sense this is my destination. I buy a piece of land and in a strong reflection of the sun I catch a glimpse of the building I'm to build there. I seem to receive commands coming from somewhere very deep inside me; so unexpected that I cannot, nor do I want to, counteract. I summon architects from all over the world; I buy the finest woods; I call in carpenters and artists of all kinds: the embellishment of the house never stops. The plan of the construction is circular, and precisely oriented in respect to the stars.

This building is not intended for me, nor for my children. I must wait for someone that will come from the sea; someone important for my land and my people, and for many others. I want to be ready to welcome him. I don't know who he is, or when exactly he'll arrive. The only way I can make sure I don't miss the opportunity to meet him is to host every traveler passing by. In return, I ask only that they tell me their story. Scientists, musicians, magicians, astrologers and soothsayers come and go: the house grows bigger and bigger, the memories it holds richer and richer.

My scribes transcribe everyone's story on parchments that I keep with great care, in a special space, a sort of corridor all around the circumference of the building. These tales are the most precious of all treasures. The sparkle of truth and power of all those lives will be a calling for the man I'm waiting for.

In my palace, the poor are fed and clothed, the rich housed as befits their rank.

I take deep pleasure in being able to immerse myself in so many different cultures. I no longer feel the need to move all the time. However, I often go to the sea; it's my friend and advisor; I share all my plans and what I'm gradually understanding about this great project. As it grows, I see it taking an increasingly clear direction.

Word spreads of my hospitality, tales and legends are born; I am spoken of as a king. This makes me smile and also gives me great pleasure. Listening to all these stories I realized that true nobility is that of the heart, true privilege is to understand the purpose of one's life. I think I have both. My soul is serene, and I feel a great sense of accomplishment. I know I'll never meet the man I am waiting for, but the house will be like a beacon to direct his arrival, his birth, further down the line of time.

Many years pass. One evening, while talking to the sea, I see a ship dock and someone from the bow beckoning me to come aboard. I suddenly feel young again, and the desire to sail away overwhelms me: that's how I leave my body.

2
FROM LIFE TO LIFE

2.1 Simultaneous Lives

The idea of living more than one existence, today, is no longer just exclusive to mystical groups or Eastern philosophies. More and more people are aware they've lived at other points in time. Universities and scientific centers studying this phenomenon are present all over the world.

Scientific theories of time suggest that the flowing from past to future is the effect of our senses, but not the real nature of time, which is still mysterious. The past, the future, and therefore the present as their point of conjunction do not exist separately; there is a single now in which all events are simultaneous and connected: a sphere of time, in which everything is present and in a constantly entangled and coordinated motion. The future could then modify the past, effects could manifest before their causes: our sensory reality created by three dimensions plus the perception of time is still an unfolding game, until the movement of the sphere stops.

That point will have such complexity that our universe itself and all its components will become something completely different and multi-dimensional.

If time as we perceive it is an illusion, and we have multiple existences in the sphere of time, thinking of them as past is too easy a way to approach the issue. Our presence in time is not linear, but each one of our dives into time—each incarnation—is simultaneous with all the others. Your main point of awareness now is connected to the physical body you inhabit at this moment, and to all the information your brain processes about the stimuli your senses bring to it.

Yet, your cells are made of the same stuff as the stars, and in them is the potential to connect to everything they've recorded in their long journey through the universe, to all their transformations, and to every moment in time. Underlying the research and stories presented in this book, there is the conviction that each cell has the potential to also connect to memories in other bodies, at other points in time, yet animated by the same node of awareness, outside the dimension of time.

2.2 The Central Pivot

The point in time where you have the most power is always the one where you are most present. That is, the moment from which you can change the balance between your lives, and increase your awareness, is in the space-time stage where you are now.

This is one of the reasons we don't fully remember our lives at other points in time. Being aware of our extension in time, when supported by an intimate balance and a desire to improve oneself, is a critical step in achieving spiritual wholeness. But a complete remembrance, without first building our personality and achieving some understanding of our role in the world, could be counterproductive to our happiness and growth. We might become deeply absorbed in memories, sensations and feelings of other times; perhaps from lives so intense that we forget that our playing field is the existence we have now. Or we might lose the pleasure of exploring it.

On the contrary, when we're genuinely interested in becoming the best and most complete version of ourselves, to be of service to others and Life, broadening our awareness to different ways of feeling, thinking, loving—all present within us as reverberations of other points of our presence in time—helps us become more aware of our mission.

They make us stronger and take us closer to our essence as they connect to the most precious emotions we carry with us, from lifetime to lifetime. Falco Tarassaco,[1] the late founder of Damanhur, summarized this concept as follows: "*The trauma of the long journey from body to body erases superficial memories, leaving the deeper, more meaningful ones bright and intact.*"

We all are/have been woman and man, noble and servant, brave and fearful, victim and oppressor; we've had existences in different peoples, holding beliefs and values of all kinds. Accepting without judgement, that within us there are lives in which we made choices that we probably don't agree with today—or believed in ideas different from now—helps us open our minds and hearts. Tolerance and understanding can then bloom, also towards those who are different from us.

In the great Game of time, our actions in one point resonate elsewhere: the range of experiences

(1) Philosopher, painter, healer, poet and writer Falco Tarassaco (1950-2013) is the visionary inspiration and spiritual guide of Damanhur. Falco had the ability to tap into the great reservoirs of universal knowledge. His unwavering commitment to the awakening of humanity is intertwined with the experience of Damanhur. There, his message of practical idealism inspired the construction of the Temples of Humankind, a work of sacred art, a spiritual beacon for the world, built by hand in the heart of a mountain.

we choose to live—as a result of our applied awareness, or as a consequence of other choices—is broad. The time of each life is the dimension containing the events at our disposal. Each one of these events, in turn, consists of several facets, several possibilities, which allow us to choose, and ensure that fate is not fixed. But once you've chosen an outcome of the possible event—which is in fact a specific arrangement of the particles of matter composing it—subsequent events will already have an orientation.(2)

The choice of one facet thus affects the possibilities of the next facet. The same applies if we consider all existences at the same time. The more awareness we achieve in our point of presence, our today, the more we can modify the whole picture—until we become not only aware of it, but also co-creators.

2.3 Time as a Territory

To make the idea of contemporary lives simple, you can imagine time as if it were a territory, with all moments present contemporaneously. You're probably not in front of the Taj Mahal in India right now, or in Italy under the Tower of Pisa, but you have no trouble believing that they exist at this very moment. If you've been there, you can easily recall

(2) *See page 199.*

memories and sensations of that time: whether it was a rainy or sunny day, whether it was day or night, who you were with, perhaps even the scents in the air and the sounds around you...

If time were also a territory, you could then easily imagine that somebody is now living in Agra around 1632, when the construction of the Taj Mahal began; the same is true for someone living now in Pisa in 1173, when work began on the tower and nobody foresaw it would tilt, becoming one of the most famous monuments of Italy.

And if you actually had/have a life there and then, your body could make you aware of sensations, important moments, the people and things you loved, and how your existence ended on that occasion. You could thus have the certainty that your being is eternal; death, when we are immersed in the dimension of linear time, is a passage back to our "node of consciousness."

2.4 Time Trails

Elaborating on the previous example, and considering time as a territory, you could choose to go first to India and then to Italy, because these two territories exist simultaneously. Wherever you are in the world, you are not obliged to go from the destination geographically closest to you now to the one furthest away. The choice of where to go first would depend on your inclinations and the resources available to you.

In the same way, lives at points in time that predate the one in which we live today don't follow a line from the past to the present day. Lives do not start in prehistory to direct towards today, moving on from era to era. Rather, as we evolve, we are directed to peoples and civilizations that are more complex, richer in values, art and culture, wherever they are in the fabric of time. We incarnate under conditions that make us freer to make choices, to follow our hearts and the voice of our souls, and be an example and inspiration to others, until we can choose to keep coming back just to help humanity evolve.

Furthermore, in the view of the spiritual school I've chosen, we don't incarnate first as animals and then as human beings. Our soul, that node of consciousness outside of time—the vibrational field of energy and information that second by second keeps us in existence with the same identity despite the constant transformations of our body and mind—includes also plant and animal beings, simultaneously. And probably crystal beings as well, although it's more complicated to be aware of this, as they experience life and time in a very different way.

Every time we feed on a being of the earth, we feed on ourselves; every time we cut down a tree or kill an animal, it's a part of us that dies. If these actions are carried out with cruelty or lack of conscience, all of humanity becomes spiritually impoverished. Living a whole and joyful life becomes increasingly difficult for all of us.

2.5 The Web of Lives

Each of our lives, each point of presence connected to a moment in time, is in turn linked to other existences; the network of interrelations grows larger and larger, until we can imagine that we all share the same experiences. From our temporal vantage point, we can connect to every person that we were in a past life, and, of course, those people have past lives of their own. In turn, for each one of them we are potentially a future life.

Potentially because when we are within the flow of time, the future is determined only when the whole Game of lives is over, when the whole sphere of time has reached sufficient complexity to transcend the connection with matter. We are all emanations of a greater, higher Consciousness that, through us, experiences this portion of reality, our world. The Earth is a space-time stage, and we can easily assume that there are other worlds and dimensions, other forms of consciousness.

Each of us is a cell in the body of humanity. One cell dies and is replaced by another, with the same function, and so the body continues to live. There is an intelligence that permeates every single cell; it gives it its specific function, in connection with all others. Even if your body dies, the element you represent, your function, is always present.

The field of energy and information that now vibrates in you, returns in a new body, in another existence. There will be a new observer, participating in shaping reality with their attention. Again and again, for all of us, until the whole Game of Lives is complete.

3
THE EMBROIDERY OF TIME

3.1 A Puzzle of Presence

We are all cells of the same humanity, the experiences of each of us feed the reservoir of our species. Their value to others is as great as our awareness as we're living them. We've all had many existences: the story of our soul is a puzzle of presences. Today, in this age of Awakening, each tassel can find its right fit to increase our awareness of who we are and the meaning of this existence, until we fully comprehend that what we can call our true self is at the point of connection between all these experiences. It's a point of presence outside of time, for which all lives are simultaneous. We are a network of energy and information, with a central node connecting the divine presence that animates us to the events we encounter when we are immersed in time and in form—on our planet or elsewhere.

Each of us has probabilities and possibilities to combine and play in different planes of existence and lives within the material plane, inventing strategies and participating as if it were a Game. Time is both the dimension of, and the support to this great Game, with possibilities and talents to mix in different lives. We play them all, all at once.

Perhaps our true nature is precisely that of time-beings, beings that are aware of their presence in multiple moments of time. We might then reclaim parts of ourselves—and of our consciousness—to expand our understanding of what living means: it's not just inhabiting our bodies and feeling like a monad separate from others, confined by the extent of our skin. Our thoughts, emotions and dreams take us far beyond our physical boundaries, and even our bodies are not one single units.

You're composed of approximately 30 trillion cells, of different ages and with different experiences. Your body, therefore, is a community. And so is your soul, which attracts in its field different aspects that you can contact and integrate, to experience life with greater presence and awareness. These aspects are facets to welcome with love and gentleness, to enter into communion with your divine nature, and learn to open up to the larger community of Life, Earth, animals, plants, subtle and spiritual forces.

The more you are able to hear the different voices that make up the song of your soul, the more you can hear those of other humans and all the beings sharing the Planet with you.

If you don't just identify with who you are now, you can live with more confidence, feeling that there is a greater purpose for life, and it has a direction. That direction is evolution: knowing that we all have lived, or rather are living, at different points in time gives us more perspective and power to make the choices that can make a difference now. These are special times for all of humanity. To avoid our own extinction we must begin to truly care for each other and our planet, to feel like one great Being.

3.2 What's Happening to Earth?

Earth is already changing frequency. The Schumann resonance, i.e. the vibrating electromagnetic field surrounding our planet that operated on an extremely low frequency of 7.83 Hz for eons, is spiking often way beyond that. As a Sentient Being, Earth herself is going through her own process of elevation and transformation.

The recent scientific string and superstring theories, that attempt to merge quantum mechanics with Albert Einstein's general theory of relativity, hypothesize that everything in this universe is essentially strings, that is one dimensional objects, vibrating in different ways. The same concept is found in the Veda, the ancient sacred Hindu texts: "*Everything that happens in our life is linked to our vibrating universe.*" And the Kybalion, the fundamental texts of Egypt-derived hermetic doctrines, says: "*Differences between the various manifestations of the universal power are due entirely to the varying rate and mode of vibrations.*"

If Earth is transforming, following an impulse from the universe, we can experience this mutation with her. If we guide it with awareness through our free will, it can lead us to a new future. Allied to all the living forces of the Earth and the spiritual energies supporting our evolution, we humans must take the first, indispensable step: connecting and feeling like one great humanity, moving from "I" to "We." Only in this way, will we be able to feel one with others, experiencing unity in multiplicity, exalted by sharing with others, not by lessening them.

All the lives we have collected, all that we have experienced has prepared us for the evolutionary transition we are facing today. A momentous change that offers us extraordinary opportunities, and also requires plenty of courage to let go of all the old systems, and open like a flower to a new light.

3.3 Identity or Download?

For many years I have been fascinated by the work of the Bruce Lipton, whose groundbreaking studies on epigenetics have expanded towards a bio-spiritual model of human life.

Lipton states that our identity is not within us, rather we are electromagnetic antennas. Our body is like a television set receiving an incoming broadcast from a greater field of intelligence. Our identity is captured, moment by moment, by protein antennas on the surface of ourselves. In this vision, we make a continuous download of ourselves; we are constantly transmitted to our body. The signal comes from a field of energy and information much more complex than our individuality(3).

(3) The possibility of transferring information without physical transmission is demonstrated by IBM quantum computers, whose second generation is already under study. Instead of relying on a sequence of 0's and 1's like a traditional computer—0 and 1 representing well-defined values—quantum computers accept the principle of indetermination, also known as the "observer's effect." According to this principle, identity is a probability within a spectrum and values cannot be established a priori, as reality changes as an effect of being observed. The possibilities of computation are therefore infinite. The channel for teleportation—the non-physical transmission of information—is possible because entanglement through space and time means that when you change something on one particle, it can have an impact on the other. *See Chapter 5 for an in-depth discussion of these concepts.*

A similar approach is found in the studies of Fred Alan Wolf, an American theoretical physicist specializing in quantum physics, and in the relationship between physics and consciousness. Wolf argues that our identity is not given by material neurophysiological processes in the body and the brain, but rather by something that animates and permeates them, coming from a level of reality that is not material.

Our body can function electrically, neurologically, physically, but the "real" person seems to be something "outside" these processes. If the level of reality we experience with our senses were all of reality, then physiology could explain every phenomenon, but quantum physics has proven the existence of a more fundamental dimension of matter.

We can assume that consciousness is not based on something material: there is no evidence that there is a "person" inside of us. We use a name to define who we are, but we are not that name. If we look at a picture of ourselves from many years ago we recognize ourselves, even though our face is very different from how we appear in the mirror today. What holds our identity together—given that the cells in our brains, and not just those in our organs, tissues and bones—are also regenerating periodically?

In a 2021 interview,[4] Wolf said: "*When I look at the way neurons work, I come to the conclusion that the emission of neurotransmitters from synaptic vesicles in the brain is probabilistic, and seems to fit very well into a picture that is consistent with quantum physics. One of the chief elements of a possible connection between quantum physics and the body would seem to be found in the observer effect of quantum physics, that has not been taken into consideration by any of the classical neuro-physiological models. It is the ability by which one can move, change or cause a series of events to occur, by performing acts of observations. One can actually affect or disrupt the state of the object being observed.*

Intent in this case would give the possibility of determining where the observed particle is located— that is, the collapse of the wave function in quantum terms. This would correspond to which event will take place among multiple possibilities along a given trajectory that cannot be explained in a mechanistic way.[5]

(4) Fred Alan Wolf, *What is the Nature of Personal Identity*, https://www.closertotruth.com/series/what-the-nature-personal-identity#video-3969, 2021.

(5) Wolf refers to the quantum Zeno effect, also known as the Turing paradox: a feature of quantum-mechanical systems allowing a particle's time evolution to be arrested by measuring it frequently enough with respect to some chosen measurement setting.

When atoms interact, they follow the laws of quantum mechanics, which predict possibilities multiplying into possibilities, but when an observer interacts with what is going on, it narrows the field down. In this way, certain possibilities no longer occur. If you observe a quantum system a number of times, you can actually alter the path by which that system evolves.

Evolution is not just a random process, it's a directed process through the observer effect. Some say that you could have the same effect in a materialistic world, except that we need to ask: where's the observer?

This process cannot be explained with one material thing interacting with another; what is making the process can't be matter. If it were matter, it would lead to an endless multiplication of probabilities. But if there's a narrowing, a focus that is forming, then there has to be a non-material focuser."

3.4 The Frequency of Violet

If time does not exist or is all present, and our identity is a transmission we receive, "creating" us again and again, then the specific transmission band to which each of us is connected could also be active in other points of the sphere of time.

The broadcast is always active, the container in which it is downloaded changes: in each existence we have a different body receiving the signal, and a different "observer."

Our true self, then, might be at the point of connection between all experiences; a crystal of consciousness of which each life is a different facet, and all are simultaneous. That is also the point of origin of each of our observers.

If the transmission we tune into in every lifetime is the same, then each of our existences has a common vibration: the one coming from that node of consciousness outside of time. What changes is the stage, which gives us different circumstances and possibilities to refine our essence.

To give a colorful example, if your node of presence is violet, you'll have the frequency of violet in each of your lives; in every existence you'll explore a nuance of it, a particular shade, until you grasp the full extent of the potential of violet, and distil its maximum purity.

The goal is to donate the result of your experiences to Life and to others, and enrich the wisdom of all humanity. Indeed, we don't only receive, we also broadcast.

We are actual transceivers: our thoughts and states of consciousness influence the environment around us. We can close our door, but the vibrational field around us still reaches us, and our own emanations reach others. We are all fish in the same aquarium, and the bubbles we emit create a pattern affecting all beings in our space.

This phenomenon is proven by new diagnostic tools, such as magneto-encephalography that uses probes outside the head to read brain activity Thoughts are transmitted in space.

Positive thoughts towards oneself and others emit coherent, constructive frequencies that can intertwine with those of others, and create a common orientation and a loving field. In this way, antenna receptors become increasingly focused on higher vibrational frequencies that help us live with greater harmony and consciousness.

Cognitive science and the study of how the brain works have shown that all thoughts are based on interpretations of memories: if we embrace memories that are broader than just one context and one lifetime, we can be wiser and more generous. Wisdom gives understanding, acceptance, and the ability to forgive others and ourselves; this fills the field of the now with constructive frequencies, and cleans up the past with loving interpretations.

The Christ's teaching "love thy neighbor as thyself" is therefore a veritable formula for individual and collective happiness and well-being. It gives a direction on how you can become your violet frequency—or whatever your personal color is—at its most fulfilled, complete and radiant self.

4
A GAME STILL IN PROGRESS

4.1 The Absolute and the Fragments of Time

In the thought of the great seventeenth-century philosopher Baruch Spinoza, who also had an important influence on Albert Einstein, there is no separation between the material and the spiritual. The same concept is key to many Eastern philosophies and to the philosophy of Damanhur that inspires my reflections. The absolute is in everything. This should reassure us that whatever happens is part of a greater plan, and maybe everything always ends well no matter what.

The perfect balance, the complete divinization of everything, though, is not found in the different fragments of space-time, but only in the whole. In our little piece of the universe, on the plane of material reality that, however illusory, defines much of our perception, the game is still open, the outcome still in doubt. There are several lines of probability to the future: not all of them lead to a world in which it will be easy to live and maintain our humanity.

It's paramount to take concrete, joyful and aware actions towards knowledge, union, peace, harmony with others and nature. Now.

Standing by and just watching the deterioration of society accelerating does not equal taking a neutral position. It means we have not full realized that in this epochal transition, each one of us is key in changing the fate of humanity. We need to do our best to give strength to the line of new consciousness that is emerging parallel to the negative one. Every generous action and every positive word count; every relationship permeated with awareness makes a difference.

We cannot fully comprehend the mysteries of the Absolute, as long as we are in a finite reality: however, we can choose to trust that there is a greater Design towards evolution, one that requires our participation. Its seed within us has the power to guide us like a scent showing the way to a wanderer in a starless night. Every human being is an electro-magnetic antenna: something in us is predisposed to receive impulses coming from spiritual energies that participate in a more conscious way in the design of the Absolute.

4.2 Broadcast Glitches

What if, in addition to picking up the evolutionary frequencies of the universe, we also had receptors for signals coming from multidimensional, complex and conflicting fields outside of us? What if the battle we often have within us—and those of nations against nations—were a mirror image of a greater war? We could assume there is a signal set up to ignite aggressive instincts, and push us toward ever greater disunity. It would be a memory-trap, misleading as to where the battleground really is. This is not a new theme: there's a great Matrix that is part of an even greater scheme in our galaxy. A sort of Star Wars in which our planet, so rich in life and diversity plays a key role.

In a battle of this kind, the shield of planetary protection is not technological, but given by the elevation of our consciousness and the cohesiveness of our spiritual field. It's only strong enough if it's unified, if we can make ourselves whole, and connect with love to others. Putting our memories in order, creating a map of our presence in time helps us orient towards the values we want to embody; we can receive a cleaner signal, with less interference stirring emotions and creating inner turmoil. This is the time to connect to the positive characteristics of each of our lives, understand and forgive every mistake we made.

Knowing who we are, and choosing to create a new humanity together with others, will finally make us feel complete and in the right place to enchant ourselves and the universe with a new story: that of a single direction of evolution. Being more aware of our Game across time can help us to find more meaning in the path of humanity, understand its plot and the possible turning points. Our time is always now.

4.3 The Return Signal

If we are transceivers, the outcome of our experiences reaches a field way beyond us: the source of the broadcast emits, and then receives our return signal. If the point of transmission is transcendent—a plane of consciousness higher than our own—our emissions "color" it, too. We modify it by creating an image of the world we live in. This is our collettive storytelling to the universe.

The story we've been broadcasting in the last millennia is based on a paradigm of prevarication and domination of a few on all others and nature. This is not in harmony with life. Climate change will present us with greater and greater challenges, and it won't even be enough to stop the whole world in order to overcome them, as we tried to do with the pandemic in 2020.

Nor will it be possible to build walls or barriers. Only new communities based on shared values can, little by little, create the harmony needed to grant a future to the next generations.

This epoch can be a time for global rehearsal in solidarity and transformation. We can awaken the feeling of being just one humanity, and move in the opposite direction of globalization and war. We need a complete re-design: if we can imagine it, we can turn it into a reality, as manifestation always follows intention, matter always obeys consciousness. A new quest for the true meaning of being human, and what's worth living for.

The American philosopher Charles Eisenstein ponders in a poignant video interview:[6] *"What's a new story that can make sense of a world that is disintegrating into senselessness? ...*

It is understanding that my purpose here actually is not to maximize my safety, security, wealth, or self-interest. My purpose here, and the reason that I am on Earth and in this cosmos, is that I carry gifts that I yearn to express, to give to the world, just like every species, just like every being.

(6) Charles Eisenstein, *And the music played the band*, YouTube, January 2022.

There's no species in an ecosystem that only takes and degrades the ecosystem. Every species actually contributes to the aliveness of the collective, to the unfolding of life and beauty.

... It doesn't look like that right now, that we are a gift to life and beauty on Earth, does it? But that is what a mature species becomes. And part of the transition that we are in right now is simply the maturation of the human species. And it's true on the individual level as well."

Awakening the memories of other you's at different points in time, can help you become aware of all your talents and the full extent of your being. You can then truly see yourself as a "gift" embroidering life on the fabric of time. There are certainly wise voices within you, to help you better understand the events of these times, and overcome moments of collective panic with a multi-dimensional historical perspective: inner treasures distilled through the unfolding of entire existences.

5
AND, WHAT IS TIME?

5.1 Still a Mystery

Time is still one of the most mysterious aspects of our universe, and not only for philosophers, even for scientists. In the equations of Isaac Newton,—alchemist and scientist born in the mid-seventeenth century, founder of classical mechanics, of the theory of universal gravitation and inventor of infinitesimal calculus—time was always present, but today in the fundamental equations of physics it is no longer there. Many scientists wonder if time really exists, or if it is only the result of our perception.

After Newton, who formulated his theories between 1600 and 1700, it was Albert Einstein who revolutionized the understanding of the concept of time. According to his Theory of Relativity, published in 1905, past, present and future cannot be clearly and unequivocally separated. The future is as real and determined as the present and the past. There's a higher intelligence, a God that permeates every aspect of existence, a "legitimate harmony of all that exists," extending beyond what we can perceive in the world, sustaining the complexity of the whole Design.

According to Einstein, time is a reality, but the perception of its flow is "only an illusion, albeit a very persistent one." Just as the frames of an old movie all exist on film, all moments of time already exist. The projector illuminates one frame after another, just as we perceive one event after another, but there is no physical law selecting one "now" over another. It's only our perception indicating that things change, but time could be compared to a frozen river, on which you can theoretically move in all directions. From this perspective, each of our actions continues to exist as part of the static whole. The thoughts we had five minutes ago, or the actions we performed years ago, remain embedded in the fabric of space-time.

5.2 Space-Time

Albert Einstein demonstrated that time is not an absolute, but it's relative to speed and position. Time doesn't flow for everyone in the same way. Depending on the circumstances, time flows slower or faster: if we could travel at the speed of light, our mass would be equal to the entire universe and time would freeze in a static singularity[7] like the center of a spinning wheel. And on a distant planet, the "present" moment would not be the same present we experience here, just as the starlight we see sometimes reaches us from suns that no longer even exist. Moreover, not only is the present moment not the same at different points in the universe, it also has different durations. At the edge of the universe our present moment might last 100,000 years.

Just as there are different times at different points in the universe—as the atomic clocks of GPS satellites prove—the Earth herself has different times. If, when the Earth was formed, two perfectly synchronized clocks had been placed, one in the core of the planet and one on its surface, today they would mark different dates: the one at the center of the Earth would be 2 and a half years behind. The core of our planet is therefore 2.5 years younger than the crust: the position within a gravitational field modifies the relative speed of time.

The same calculation has been made for the Sun: considering the enormous mass of our star,

(7) A singularity is a point at which a function takes an infinite value, especially in space–time when matter is infinitely dense, such as at the centre of a black hole.

calculations suggest that between its younger center and its surface, the age difference is now 40,000 years. Time is therefore inseparable from space: it depends on the mass present in the point of the universe where we are, and our speed. Space and time are relative and interdependent physical quantities that create a single quantity, called space-time or chronotope.

5.3 Time Does not Exist

Not all scientists agree on the concept of space-time. The idea of chronotope is now being challenged by Julian Barbour, an English physicist, who argues that time is nothing but change. What we perceive as what's happening around us is change, not time. Barbour presents calculations and theories that support the structure of a timeless universe: space exists, but time is not necessary to explain reality.

Barbour also questions the "arrow of time," a foundational theory related to the Second Law of Thermodynamics, or the Law of Entropy. According to this law, the degree of disorder in an isolated system increases with time in a spontaneously irreversible way. However, recent research has demonstrated that, working at molecular scales and over extremely short periods of time, things can take place in either direction: in a very small space entropy can sometimes decrease rather than increase, but the effect lasts only a tiny interval of time. Life itself is a temporary reversal of entropy; it's order out of randomness, but it requires an input of energy. And then, at a certain point the system begins to break down again, returning to disorder. At a macroscopic level, therefore, entropy has been used to indicate the direction in which time is moving: the further into the future we look, the more disorder increases.

The Second Law of Thermodynamics is one of the foundations of modern theoretical physics, one of the few laws about which physicists feel most certain. Yet, recent research has demonstrated that, working at molecular scales and over extremely short periods of time, things can take place in either direction: in a very small space entropy can sometimes decrease rather than increase, even though the effect lasts only a tiny interval of time.

In *The Janus Point*, written in 2020, Barbour proclaims his opposition to the Arrow of Time theory, arguing that the second law has been misapplied, and that it's actually the growth of order that determines the experience of time.

From his perspective, the Big Bang is the "Janus Point," a moment of minimal order from which time could flow, and order increase, in two directions. While most physicists predict that the universe is moving toward disorder, Barbour sees the possibility for order—the stuff of life—to grow without limit.

Before Barbour, as early as the 1980's, British cosmologist Sir Fred Hoyle[(8)] in *The Intelligent Universe*[(9)] theorized a universe whose direction was that of ever increasing order. Hoyle imagined that wave functions or information from the past could meet with equivalents from the future, and thus determine which event would manifest on the plane of reality under consideration: "*If events could operate not only from past to future, but also from future to past, the seemingly intractable problem of quantum uncertainty could be solved. Instead of living matter becoming more and more disorganized, it could react to quantum signals from the future—the information necessary for the development of life. Instead of the Universe*

(8) Sir Fred Hoyle, 1915-2001, is also known because he coined the term "Big Bang" to disprove the theory that the universe originated from a large explosion. Hoyle was convinced that panspermia was at the origin of life on Earth.

(9) The intelligent universe, Michael Joseph Ltd Publishing,1983.

committed to increasing disorder and decay, the opposite could then be true."

5.4 Our Senses and the Flow of Time

If from the immensely large—our universe—we move to the infinitely small and take into account quantum physics, the notion of time doesn't exist; time isn't even one of the variables used in the equations. In the quantum world, a system can be in a combination of several different states, which makes the direction of time unclear. At least in theory, its evolution is simultaneous in two opposite directions, either forward or backward in time. Only the presence of an observer can determine which state you are in, and in which direction you are moving.

This is true not only at the microscopic level, but also in our daily experience, argues Italian physicist Carlo Rovelli. In *The Order of Time*(10) Rovelli suggests that our perception of the flow of time depends on our perspective, which is defined more by our brain structure and emotions than by the actual physical universe. The laws of physics are mathematical equations used to describe the universe—from the behavior of atoms to galaxies—and no law says that events need only unfold

(10) Carlo Rovelli, *The Order of Time*, Riverhead Books, 2017.

in one direction. All equations are unrelated to the arrow of time, and would also work in the backward direction of time.

And if past and future no longer oppose each other, then also the present necessarily cannot exist, and time disappears: there's a contradiction between the laws of physics that are reversible, and our life that seems irreversible. According to physicists, we live in an approximation of reality, and we share the perception of a "bubble" of time, which we call the present.

Our understanding of the world is therefore based on a sequence of events, with physical reality existing only in the moment we perceive as present. From the present, we can move with our minds and emotions into the past, but always from a "now" that immediately no longer exists. This perception is reinforced by the fact that thought has a linguistic basis, and most of the languages used today bind us to describe every event as actions placed in time, with a beginning and an end.

5.5 How to Tie Everything Together?

To understand the theoretical framework that allows us to think about contemporary lives, we can consider time as Gnomo Orzo describes it in *I Make Things Happen:*[11] "*a great ocean in which every tiny drop of water is an event. This image of one vast coherent fabric is the same as Albert Einstein's Theory of Relativity. And as every ship that crosses the ocean can take different routes, so it happens to all of us. At least once in our lives we've experienced miracles, incredible difficulties, small or large strangeness, events that have taken precise directions in a totally irrational way and that we hastily labeled as 'random events.'*

These events, perhaps, were warning us that our beliefs about time are too limited to do justice to such a complex phenomenon. That river flowing from the past to the future, which as children we were taught to call 'time,' looks more and more like one of the many underwater currents of a vast ocean connecting all waters and lands."

If the ocean of time connects all waters and lands, then all of your points of presence in time are also connected by a thread of energy, the singular vibration of your soul experiencing the world of form in so many different ways. And through your senses, and the memories that your body

(11) *I Make Things Happen*: *Selfica, A Technology for the Third Millenium*, DHORA, 2021.

still holds— or rather to which it can tune in as if it were a living antenna—you can shift your awareness to other points in time.

Time, in this sense, does not exist, and simultaneously everything is always present. A paradox you can comprehend only with those parts of you that transcend your identification with your current self, feeling part of a single Consciousness that permeates every atom of matter and every instant of time.

5.6 The Entanglement of Lives

Entanglement is a fundamental phenomenon of quantum physics, still largely mysterious. According to it, the quantum state of each constituent of a quantum system depends instantaneously on the state of the other constituents. This bonding is maintained even when the particles are at very large distances, and has surprising, non-intuitive, experimentally verified consequences.

This interaction at a distance, which Einstein never accepted, was discovered in 1926 by another Austrian physicist, Erwin Schrödinger—the one who coined the term entanglement—through the wave equation, which is independent of time.

Gnomo Orzo explains: "*The wave equation of a particle is threefold: there is an equation for the particle that sends the message; another for the particle that receives the message; and a third that represents both particles when they were still one. Einstein considered this quantum correlation to state that if two or more particles can communicate instantaneously, it would be a violation of the constant of the speed of light in the universe.*

Considering that the constant of the speed of light has been proven on every circumstance, Einstein argued there were hidden variables in quantum mechanics that made it a flawed theory. On the contrary, the Schrödinger equation—thanks to which the physicist won the Nobel Prize in Physics in 1933—illustrates that the particles in a quantum system are actually always one, a single primeval particle. Their correlation doesn't violate relativity, because it is one single particle communicating with itself, not a message that is sent to someone else. From the universal point of view, the fact that two particles have separated doesn't divide them, they are still the same. From this point of view, it's no longer communication between two separate entities, it's awareness.

As our understanding increases, the phenomena we observe in particles can also be contemplated for much more complex systems, for planets, for human beings. It is the same phenomenon on a different scale. In this perspective, the soul is a super wave equation that contemplates all its parts, which vibrate in a sympathetic way because they are part of the same system. In our soul, our node of consciousness, communication is instantaneous: that is the point where the present exists; in life inside a body, we perceive past and future, because our understanding is limited."

The aforementioned Fred Alan Wolf, in a 2021 interview, illustrates the same principle: "*When we think of communication in a mechanical way, we imagine there's some kind of particle, like a photon, that has to get from here to there. If, on the other hand, we think of 'communication' according to quantum mechanics, the brain might be a very complex quantum entanglement tool.*" (12)

As you become aware of your presence in time, according to the principle of entanglement, you don't just have a correlation, but you can access a system of greater complexity, greater consciousness. It is as if people who read the same book were not only connected by the fact that they

(12) Fred Alan Wolf, *What is the Nature of Personal Identity* https://www.closertotruth.com/series/what-the-nature-personal-identity# video-3969, 2021.

share the same notions even at a distance, but could actually unlock all the knowledge contained in the book only when they are together. When you consciously reconnect with the other parts of you across time, you can acquire more and more access to all the complexity of your soul and your Mission in the world.

6
A MAP OF LIVES

6.1 A Light that I Knew

The first impression of having already been on this planet, in a different place and time than my current existence, is full of light. Literally. I was about twenty years old and I was on a large ferry docking in Piraeus, Greece. I get seasick easily so, relieved to have finally arrived, I went up on deck to breathe, and take a look at the harbor. I was excited to put my feet on that mythical land for the first time, but I certainly didn't expect to feel transported to another space, right there on the ship.

The bright light that surrounded me seemed different from all others, yet I knew I'd seen it before, already felt it on my skin; it had already been part of my perception. That light felt not only as brightness, but as if it were a direction of the spirit, an orientation of my heart and mind that I recognized. Without understanding it at all. And so it remained just a sensation, intertwined with the myriad that first trip to Greece gave me.

I felt at home there, my love for that land was immediate and unconditional.

The following year I returned to Greece on vacation, and joined a group of new friends. They spoke English with me, but were always speaking Greek to each other. I liked that language; strangely enough it sounded almost familiar, even though I didn't understand anything... until one morning I woke up and, without realizing it, I was able to understand and answer... in Greek! Just like that. It was as if my operating system had been upgraded overnight with the addition of a new language, and its underlying logic!

It was quite a shock, but I was so happy that I didn't concentrate so much on trying to explain how it happened; I wanted to surprise my other friends who had stayed in Athens. It was a long trip, from Zakynthos to the capital, first by ferry and then on an old bus full of people, luggage, many chickens and a few goats, but it was exciting. I tried to understand fragments of sentences and reconstruct their meaning, like a crossword puzzle of sounds in my mind.

When I returned to Italy, I decided to study Greek to really learn it, but all the books I found had ancient Greek as a reference point, and I hadn't studied it at school. The Internet did not exist yet, so I had children's books sent to me, with lots of pictures and words in block letters. Thus my "formal" education began: teddy bear, cookie, bicycle...

In the following years, I returned to Greece often and fragments of memories resurfaced in some places—especially in Crete: past lives for me were logical evidence, supported by curious flashes of images and sensations, but nothing I was interested in exploring beyond the teachings I found in Eastern doctrines.

It took fifteen years for time research to become one of the focus points of my spiritual growth. In that time, I discovered my connection to Greece, to its light and history. And after that, I brought back to memory many other ramifications of my presence in time, as a man and as a woman. Reconnecting to so many parts of myself has completed me, transformed me and helped me expand more and more my way of thinking and feeling. It's a precious gift, so much so that I wanted to share my experiences and my research with others. For this reason, later on, thanks to teachers of great knowledge and spiritual stature, I learned to follow the time tracks of other people, to verify their memories and guide them towards the completion of their personal map of lives.

6.2 "Memory"

At the end of 1992, I decided to go and live in Valchiusella, in Piedmont, to participate in the spiritual and social research of Damanhur, one of the oldest and most established intentional communities in the world. During a group meditation using Selfica,(1) I heard in my mind the word "memory." It was clear it was a direction on how to proceed with greater awareness on my path.

In Damanhurian philosophy, memory is not only a recollection of events and their interpretation. It also refers to the faculty of being aware of the expansion of your being across time. It's a connection to other lives within the fabric of time, so that you can reach greater clarity on your essence and mission.

(1) Selfica is a spiritual "technology" developed at Damanhur for the expansion of consciousness. The coherent and oriented energy fields created by Selfica make it possible to move consciousness easily through time. For this reason, I use Selfic instrumentation during my seminars to help others retrieve memories of their lives at other points in time. See also: *Spirals of Energy*, by Esperide Ananas, Devodama, 2013.

From this point of view, "memory" is a sense of the soul, which combines with our other "inner" senses. They are faculties that developed in us humans when our physiological and cerebral complexity made us apt to host an active principle of awareness, a "divine spark."

This divine principle within gives us these special senses so that we can participate fully in the natural and spiritual eco-system we are immersed in—and of which we should ensure a balanced continuous transformation. Thanks to this transcendent aspect present in us, we human beings are, like some other animal species, a "bridge-form." We are a point of passage and connection between the material and spiritual planes. Our body and mind—mirror of each other and, together, a fractal of the design of the whole universe—are suitable vehicles for the experience of the absolute principle in the material world.

From this perspective, we ourselves are the "senses" of God, an absolute principle that can be that can be described as the intelligence-love that contains everything. An "unmovable motor" acquiring knowledge of itself through the countless forms and worlds into which it broke its wholeness up.

6.3 The Senses of the Soul

The divine spark bears responsibility and free will: it can make us conscious agents of the extension of the principle of Consciousness within the universe. For this reason, the inner sense most accessible to every human being is the sense of the divine. It is the awareness of our origin beyond the material dimension. It's the inner compass showing us the direction of our awakening, helping us give value and meaning to things in order to make union, beauty and connection grow.

To explore the sphere of time, the sense of memory intertwines with that of dreaming, which allows us to perceive states of being without the support of physical form. It is not simple imagination: it is the faculty to move our consciousness to different points in time and space and see, feel, perceive the events that take place there. Astral travel and lucid dreaming techniques are some of the possibilities connected to this ability. At a different level are the techniques of remote-viewing, which apparently were also used for espionage during the Cold War.

The sense of memory connected with that of dreaming makes it possible to remember/relive moments of one's existence in other points of time. To be able to do this, it's important not only to see, touch, hear, taste, smell the world around us, but to learn to transform our frequency in order to become the "things" we want to explore. We need to feel that they are really part of us, that everything is connected in a wonderful and profound order, we are not separated from. And of which we can become aware.

This feeling of being part of an intelligent and sensitive whole, with a purpose of evolution that encompasses—and goes beyond—each individual, our species and our Planet, can also be considered an inner sense. It supports the awakening and integration of all the others: it is the "sense of love." The first story of this book talks about this. It is the life offering the key to understanding all the others, in a path of recomposition and evolution through Love[(2)].

(2) In addition to the inner senses of the divine, memory, dreams and love, there are other perceptions that can be considered attributes of our divine nature: the sense of desire, understood as the faculty to direct the creative will; the sense of exchange, i.e. sharing the meaning of others' experiences; the sense of communication, understood as deep empathy and energetic connection; and the sense of justice, which provides every member of the human species with an ethical compass, beyond morals and culture.

6.4 A Memory from the Future

In the years following the meditation that pointed me to memory as my key to inner growth, I dedicated myself to composing my own personal map of time. This exploration brought me many surprises, even an encounter with a potential future me. I discovered afterwards that he was not in my past, because at the moment of the meeting, the sensations and what I perceived had no temporal references I could identify.

The first time I encountered this potential future me, the flame of a candle acted as a doorway for me to pass between the timelines, during a collective ceremony with music and dance. Suddenly, I was transported into a large room, illuminated by a soft light—although I could see no source of it. The hall had a large double door, which opened noiselessly and with great ease by placing both hands on it.

A very tall individual appeared to me; he was a male being belonging to a human race different from ours. He turned towards me and smiled slightly, making me jump with astonishment! I immediately lost contact, and found myself completely present back in the ceremony I was participating in. I took a few deep breaths to regain my composure and focused on the flame again, this time consciously looking for the passage. And, to my great happiness, I found it.

One of the large walls of the room was made of glass. Behind it, a stunning underwater landscape made me think of Atlantis. In the center of the room stood a beautiful globe. It had no pedestal, and seemed to be floating in the air. The planet represented was probably Earth, but the continents were different from what they are today. In an area off to the side I saw strange vehicles; I thought that perhaps this man was a pilot. I noticed curious objects and felt he was proud of them; I had the impression they were gifts from other civilizations.

What struck me about this first encounter was the clarity of my vision and, above all, the fact that this man was aware of my presence. So much so that he gave me the feeling of being expected. But as I saw the scene from the outside, I didn't realize it was a life of mine somewhere else in time. I lived it as an interesting episode of consciousness expansion.

6.5 My Second Encounter

A few months after this first experience, during another group meditation practice through the spiritual technology of Selfica, I felt myself morphing into this being. I saw the darkness of space all around me, and realized I was on a spaceship! It was a large vessel, so complex as to be a sentient structure, which I guided through my thought. The metals making the ship were "alive," too, as they were activated by thought, and acted as recorders and database.

On his/my left arm a large selfic bracelet made of many spirals made my forearm move and draw signs and codes in the air. In the center it had a sliding part, from which a beam for the activation of psychic powers came out. I even felt the metal endings of the bracelet become part of my bone structure, in a full and harmonious physical integration.

Then I had the sensation of traveling through space: I saw stars, planets, an iridescent space base in the shape of two interconnected tetrahedrons, and a planet-temple I felt was connected to many worlds. These were extraordinary perceptions, yet what struck me even more was feeling that this man belonged to a civilization in which everyone was telepathically connected, and fully aware of being part of a higher field of consciousness. I sensed a perfect symbiosis between everything and everyone.

I felt that every creature and the whole universe were kept cohesive by the thought of the divinity, which was a specific vibrational frequency; a unified field of coherence where all elements were indispensable and interconnected. This unexpected insight gave me the wonderful feeling of a great and profound order, making me feel part of an intelligent and sensitive whole as I had never experienced before.

After meditating on these episodes for a long time, I sent a letter to the Damanhurian group specialized in past lives research. I wanted to better understand what happened, and make sure it wasn't just the fruit of my imagination. I asked them to open the "book" of my soul tracks and verify if these memories corresponded to one of my points of presence in time.

This is a summary of their reply: "*Your intuitions are confirmed. Activation and coordination on multiple levels. Bases in the Universe. Living planets come alive, and move directed by impulses. Race chosen for their physical and mental predisposition to space and time travel. Precise roles and functions received as impulses/thoughts. They constitute one body and one mind. Group-individual. Total and complete use of personal resources.*

There is no idea of time, everything is present. It's not a past life, but a time exploration of a future life."

This confirmation made me reflect for days and days on how it was possible for me to remember a future me if, from my point of perception on the timeline, the future is still indeterminate. Then I understood that what I'd encountered was my own potential line of possibilities. In it, my current existence could link up with many others to compose this man's map of lives; a man living in a dimension in which time is all present. In this era, I'm a past life to this man, while he's a potential future to me, in spite of the fact that he's living in my past from the perspective of the chronological timeline—this, of course, if I really met him in Atlantis.

6.6 The Voice of the Heart

As we already discussed, from the perspective of linear time the progression of our incarnations doesn't necessarily move from past to future. If we live fully and grow in wisdom, love, and awareness, the Universal Intelligence guiding the Game of Lives selects for us peoples and civilizations that are more and more spiritually, artistically and socially complex, and with a deeper level of connection among people and with life.

There are many points in our past on this planet that are more advanced than the present we live today, even without considering the splendid civilizations that belong to historical cycles predating what history books teach us—and that today are considered a myth by most. A theme to ponder to understand the difference between progress and evolution. In this epoch, we are certainly developing more advanced technologies than those existing in the past of our historical cycle, but how much has our human and spiritual evolution increased?

Each of us is responsible for our own growth: only a profound connection with our soul can show us the right direction to discover and create and a more complete and happy way of being human. Awakening the memories of who we've been can ignite the desire for a new future—and the hope that we can make it real.

The world needs a new story. We all need a new story. To heal and awaken together and become masters of a better destiny for humanity. I offer the tales of this book to help you better understand who you are, embrace the best in you and overcome fear. In this way, you'll make purposeful choices and go towards others with a trusting smile. You'll hear the voice of your heart more and more, and create a life truly rich in meaning and love.

DAMANHUR

TO MAKE LIFE SACRED AGAIN

Founded in 1975 as a social and spiritual experiment, Damanhur is a Federation of Intentional Communities and a worldwide movement that inspires the lives of thousands of people committed to making a positive mark on the world.

The central part of Damanhur is located in Italy, in the pristine Valchiusella valley in the foothills of the Piedmont Alps. The six hundred citizens who live there have created a multilingual society, welcoming people from all over the world and all different peoples' cultures. Many other Damanhur citizens live in Italy and around the world, supporting its ideals and projects.

Damanhur was born on the inspiration of Falco Tarassaco, Oberto Airaudi (1950-2013). His dream of an enlightened future, shared with many other practical spiritual seekers, has turned into a real society, based on solidarity, art and culture, mutual love, and respect for life and all beings.

Damanhur has its own Constitution, schools for young children, art and craft workshops, a publishing house, a farm, organic restaurants and a renowned medical and holistic therapy center. Through seminars, campuses and conferences, Damanhur's researchers share the knowledge and experience of several decades of experimentation in many fields of human potential. Damanhurian teachers also gladly travel abroad to share their research and wisdom.

Damanhur has established a Foundation and an N.G.O with consultative status at the United Nations. The Community Federation is also a member of GEN (Global Ecovillage Network) and offers Gaia's education training programs.

The Temples of Humankind

The Temples of Humankind are the spiritual heart of Damanhur: an underground work of art carved by hand into the heart of a mountain, and called by many the Eighth Wonder of the World. In the Halls of the Temples thousands of people find inspiration and the ideal container for their spiritual practices. They connect to the Energies supporting the Awakening of humanity, while strengthening the synchronic flow of their life events and personal evolution..

Damanhur, Federation of Community
10080 Baldissero C.se (TO) - ITALY
editoria@damanhur.org
www.damanhur.org - www.thetemples.org/shop